# Healthy Living
## with
# gluten
# INTOLERANCE

Published in 2011 by Murdoch Books Pty Limited
www.murdochbooks.com.au

Murdoch Books Australia
Pier 8/9
23 Hickson Road
Millers Point NSW 2000
Phone: +61 (0) 2 8220 2000
Fax: +61 (0) 2 8220 2558

Murdoch Books UK Limited
Erico House
6th Floor North
93–99 Upper Richmond Road
Putney, London SW15 2TG
Phone: +44 (0) 20 8785 5995
Fax: +44 (0) 20 8785 5985

For Corporate Orders & Custom Publishing contact
Noel Hammond, National Business Development Manager

Publisher: Lynn Lewis
Designer: Jacqueline Richards
Food Consultants: Jayne Tancred and Toni Gumley
Photographer: Ian Hofstetter
Stylists: Jane Collins and Katy Holder
Food preparation: Joanne Kelly and Grace Campbell
Recipes by: Michelle Earl and members of the Murdoch Books Test Kitchen
Project Editor: Alice Grundy
Production: Joan Beal

National Library of Australia Cataloguing-in-Publication Data
ISBN:              978 1 74266 409 5 (pbk.)
Series:            Healthy eating.
Notes:             Includes index.
Subjects:          Gluten-free diet--Recipes
                   Cooking.
Dewey Number:      641.5638

A catalogue record for this book is available from the British Library.

Printed by 1010 Printing International Limited, PRINTED IN CHINA.

IMPORTANT: Those who might be at risk from the effects of salmonella poisoning (the elderly,
pregnant women, young children and those suffering from immune deficiency diseases)
should consult their doctor with any concerns about eating raw eggs.

OVEN GUIDE: You may find cooking times vary depending on the oven you are using.
For fan-forced ovens, as a general rule, set the oven temperature to 20°C (35°F) lower
than indicated in the recipe.

# Healthy Living
## with
# gluten
# INTOLERANCE

EASY *gluten-free*
RECIPES AND  LIFESTYLE SOLUTIONS

Introductory text by Dr Susanna Holt (PhD, Dietitian)

MURDOCH BOOKS

# contents

# Living with
## Gluten
# INTOLERANCE

A diagnosis of gluten intolerance no longer means the end of delicious foods. With the range of gluten-free products now available it's easy to follow a gluten-free diet, and with all the simple recipes in this book there are gluten-free meals for every occasion.

This book contains a broad range of tested gluten-free recipes that are relatively quick and easy to prepare, including both every day meals and treats for special occasions. Meals with a low glycaemic index (GI), which produce a relatively small rise in blood sugar after they're eaten, have been included for people who are affected by both coeliac disease and diabetes.

These recipes will appeal to the whole family; so even if only one family member requires a gluten-free diet, you won't need to prepare different meals for everyone else. Aside from saving you time, preparing meals the whole family can enjoy is particularly valuable for helping children to realise that there is no stigma attached to needing to follow a gluten-free diet.

This book contains practical advice on healthy gluten-free eating, cooking and shopping. It has been designed to provide people who need to follow a gluten-free diet, and those who cater for them, with important information about coeliac disease, dermatitis herpetiformis (DH) and wheat and/or gluten intolerance.

If you suspect you have coeliac disease, DH or wheat and/or gluten intolerance, it is important that you consult a qualified doctor for diagnosis.

Once you've been diagnosed, it's advisable to join your local coeliac or DH organization, where you'll be able to get invaluable support and practical advice and a referral to an expert dietitian. This can be particularly beneficial in the early stages after diagnosis.

# Coeliac Disease

The inner surface of the small intestine is lined with millions of tiny finger-like projections called villi, which absorb water and nutrients from digested food matter as it passes through the small intestine.

In people with untreated coeliac disease, the progressive damage to the villi can lead to various stomach and bowel problems and nutritional deficiencies.

Coeliac disease is both an autoimmune disorder (because the body's immune system causes the damage) and a digestive disease (because nutrient absorption is impaired).

# Dermatitis Herpetiformis

Dermatitis herpetiformis (DH) is an itchy, non-contagious skin condition that may take the form of small lumps (some topped by fluid-filled blisters called vesicles), hives, or a dermatitis-like rash. It is caused by gluten intolerance in genetically susceptible people and can flare up and subside, regardless of whether or not it's being treated. It tends to occur around the elbows, knees, buttocks, shoulder blades and ears and along the hairline and eyebrows.

Although less than 10% of DH sufferers have digestive symptoms suggestive of coeliac disease, most do have some degree of intestinal damage.

As with coeliac disease, DH is treated by maintaining a life-

Coeliac (pronounced *seel-ee-ak*) disease is a condition in which the immune system over-reacts to gluten, causing the villi to become inflamed and flattened, and compromising their ability to absorb water and nutrients.

long gluten-free diet. Significant improvements in the skin condition may take up to two years to occur through dietary changes alone. Prescribed medicines may bring relief relatively quickly, but are often accompanied by adverse effects.

## What's the difference between these conditions?

People with coeliac disease have a permanent life-long intolerance to gluten and they need to maintain a gluten-free diet throughout their lives in order to avoid intestinal damage and its associated complications.

Some people who don't have coeliac disease may also benefit from following a gluten-free or wheat-free diet, although unlike people with coeliac disease, they may be able to eat small amounts of gluten.

In some cases, non-coeliac gluten intolerance is caused by an allergy to wheat, wheat protein or other gluten-containing grains. In these circumstances, be aware that not all foods that are gluten-free are also wheat-free; some are made with wheat products from which the gluten has been removed, and may still contain allergenic components of the grain.

Wheat allergy usually develops in young children and disappears by the time they are of school age. Symptoms may include rashes, facial swelling and eczema, which appear soon after the food is consumed.

Hypersensitivity to gluten or wheat may also occur, via physiological mechanisms that are different in nature to allergic reactions.

If you suspect you are intolerant to wheat or gluten, it is vital that you see your doctor, so that coeliac disease can be investigated

If you have coeliac disease, your doctor may recommend testing for your close relatives too, as approximately 10% of your immediate family may also be affected.

**What to do if you think you have a gluten intolerance**

If you think that you may have coeliac disease, it's important that you keep eating gluten-containing foods, such as regular bread, breakfast cereals and pasta, until the relevant medical investigations have been completed. If you stop eating gluten before being tested, your blood tests and biopsy may suggest that you don't have coeliac disease even if you do (a false negative result). If you've adopted a gluten-free diet before being tested for coeliac disease, you'll need to eat gluten-containing foods again for at least six weeks before undergoing the diagnostic tests. You may suffer some symptoms during this time, but your doctor won't be able to diagnose or rule out coeliac disease unless you've been eating gluten before the tests are performed.

and either diagnosed or ruled out. If coeliac disease is not present, you may need to undergo an elimination diet in order to identify the cause of your symptoms. This should only be performed under the supervision of your health professional, especially if the patient is a child.

## How is coeliac disease diagnosed?

It can be difficult for doctors to diagnose coeliac disease because the symptoms can be vague, or similar to those of other diseases, such as irritable bowel syndrome, Crohn's disease, diverticulitis, intestinal infections, iron-deficiency anaemia and chronic fatigue syndrome. Doctors may perform tests to rule out these conditions before they consider the possibility of coeliac disease. Consequently, it can take months or years before a person is properly diagnosed with coeliac disease. However, increased education and better diagnostic tests will make it easier for doctors to diagnose coeliac disease in the future. Coeliac organizations in many countries run educational campaigns to try to increase health professionals' awareness of the condition. You should inform your doctor if you have a family history of coeliac disease, particularly if you also suffer from any of the associated symptoms.

At the moment, a biopsy of the small intestine is necessary to diagnose coeliac disease because, although blood tests can indicate that the condition may be present, their results are not perfect and cannot be relied on. People without coeliac disease can sometimes have high levels of antibodies in their blood (a false positive result) and people with the condition can sometimes have low levels of antibodies (a false negative result).

## Three steps to diagnosis:

**1** The first step is to discuss your concerns and symptoms with your doctor.

**2** If your doctor suspects coeliac disease, you will need to have a blood test to check for the presence of certain antibodies that tend to be present in higher levels in people with untreated coeliac disease. These may include anti-tissue transglutaminase antibodies (tTG), deamidated gliadin peptide immunoglobulins (DGP IgA and IgG), and endomysial antibodies (EMA).

**3** If your doctor feels that there is a chance that you have coeliac disease on the basis of your blood test and/or your symptoms, you will be referred to a gastroenterologist for a biopsy of your small intestine. To perform the biopsy, the gastroenterologist gradually eases a long flexible tube (endoscope) through your mouth down into your small intestine; this procedure is performed using local anaesthetic to minimise discomfort and patients often report that it wasn't as uncomfortable as they were expecting it to be. A tiny instrument is passed through the endoscope to collect a small tissue sample from your small intestine. If the tissue abnormalities that occur with coeliac disease (inflammation and damaged villi) are found in the sample, the gastroenterologist or your doctor will inform you that you have coeliac disease.

In cases where biopsy results are insufficient to confirm whether you have coeliac disease, your doctor may also initiate genetic testing, which can rule out the condition in some people.

## What causes coeliac disease?

Some people are born with a genetic predisposition to coeliac disease, however only around one in every 30 people with the "coeliac genes" goes on to develop the condition.

If you have coeliac disease, your doctor may recommend testing for your close relatives too, as approximately 10% of your immediate family may also be affected.

Environmental and lifestyle factors also play a role, and coeliac disease may only become active for the first time after a person experiences a period of physical or emotional stress, such as pregnancy, childbirth, surgery, bereavement, or a viral infection.

# How common is it?

For many years, coeliac disease was thought to be relatively uncommon. However, recent studies have indicated that it may affect around 1% of the population in Western countries. It is most prevalent in people of European descent (particularly among the Irish). Coeliac disease also appears to be more common in parts of Africa, South America and Asia than previously believed. Many people have never been diagnosed and consequently are untreated.

There are strong links between coeliac disease and a number of other health conditions. For example, up to 10% of people with Type 1 diabetes may also have coeliac disease and as many as 4–17% of people with Down's syndrome have coeliac disease or gluten sensitivity.

# What are the symptoms of coeliac disease?

The damaged small intestine in people with untreated coeliac disease has a reduced ability to absorb water and nutrients from food. Consequently, people with coeliac disease can experience abdominal bloating and painful cramps after eating a gluten-containing meal. Unabsorbed food matter passes from the small into the large intestine, and can cause diarrhoea, large smelly stools or (less commonly) constipation. Increased flatulence is also a common problem because bacteria that are naturally present in the large intestine can ferment the fibre and starch in the unabsorbed food matter.

Reasons that coeliac disease affects everyone differently are thought to include the length of time an individual was breast-fed (in general, it appears that the longer a person is breast-fed as a baby, the longer it takes for their symptoms to develop); the age that gluten-containing foods are first eaten; the amount of gluten in the diet; and differences in the body's sensitivity to gluten.

The severity of the symptoms experienced does not always reflect the amount of intestinal damage present, and those with the greatest degree of intestinal damage do not necessarily experience the worst symptoms. Conversely, people without symptoms still suffer intestinal damage if they eat gluten, and are still at risk of developing related problems.

A prompt diagnosis is important. The longer your coeliac disease goes undiagnosed and untreated, the greater your chance of developing nutrient deficiencies and other complications. In

It's essential that you find an experienced dietitian to help you learn to identify gluten-free foods and correct any nutritional deficiencies you may have developed while your condition was undiagnosed.

children, suspected coeliac disease should be investigated without delay; poor nutrition can cause serious developmental problems, such as delayed growth and behavioural and learning difficulties.

## Related health problems and complications

Lactose intolerance is common in people with undiagnosed and newly diagnosed coeliac disease, because the damaged gut is unable to break down lactose (the sugar in cow's milk), resulting in symptoms such as abdominal pain and bloating after milk or dairy products are consumed. This situation is usually temporary, and those affected tend to be able to tolerate dairy foods again after gluten has been avoided for a while.

People with untreated coeliac disease have a small increased risk of intestinal cancer (lymphoma and adenocarcinoma), but this elevated risk is reduced after a gluten-free diet has been maintained for some time.

People with coeliac disease also have an increased risk of other autoimmune diseases including Type 1 diabetes, hypothyroidism (an under-active thyroid), and alopecia, and there is a strong link with some genetic disorders (including Down's syndrome and Turner's syndrome).

The impaired food absorption that occurs in coeliac disease can result in deficiencies of a number of nutrients. Decreased absorption of iron, folate and vitamin B12 can lead to anaemia, which makes sufferers feel tired and possibly also irritable and depressed. People with a severely damaged small intestine may not absorb oils, fat-soluble vitamins (vitamins A, D, E and K), zinc or protein properly, resulting in weight loss, impaired growth in children, fatigue, and sometimes miscarriages, infertility and other problems. Decreased calcium absorption places people with coeliac disease at an increased risk of low bone mineral density (osteopaenia) and osteoporosis (weakened bones that are more susceptible to breaking). Improvements in all these conditions may be noted after the implementation of a gluten-free diet.

## Available treatments

The only treatment for coeliac disease and DH is to follow a gluten-free diet for life. Eating any gluten, no matter how small an amount, can damage the small intestine in people with coeliac disease, even if it doesn't cause any noticeable symptoms. Similarly, even tiny amounts of gluten can cause DH to flare up again and stop the skin from healing.

One of the best things you can do to learn about your new dietary requirements is to join your local coeliac disease or DH support organization, which can provide you with excellent practical information about how to best manage your condition and where to find gluten-free foods. They also often offer other forms of support for their members, including supermarket tours, educational talks, magazines and referral to expert dietitians. (You'll find a list of support organizations on page 189 of this book, or alternatively, search the internet or phone directory, or ask your doctor for contact information).

If you care for someone with coeliac disease or DH, such as a child or elderly relative, then you should also attend any dietary consultations with them and join your local coeliac organization for valuable support and education.

After starting a gluten-free diet, most people with coeliac disease quickly feel much better, though for other people (especially those with DH) the symptoms can linger.

Even if your symptoms take time to resolve, it's important to remember that as soon as you remove gluten from your diet, your body can start to heal. The adult small intestine is usually significantly or completely healed within 2-5 years of adopting a gluten-free diet, and healing may occur more quickly in younger people.

Initially it may be challenging to switch to a gluten-free diet and come to terms with your condition, it's important to remember that compared to the treatment of many other health conditions, following a gluten-free diet is easy.

Thanks to the growing number of people with coeliac disease, there are lots of resources available and an increasing range of gluten-free convenience foods to choose from. It is becoming easier to find safe gluten-free foods in supermarkets and health-food stores, or you can order them from specialist food companies over the internet.

Although it may seem difficult at first, with time, you'll find that eating a gluten-free diet comes naturally.

Even if your symptoms take time to resolve, it's important to remember that as soon as you remove gluten from your diet, your body can start to heal

## If symptoms don't improve

Although it's rare, some people with coeliac disease show no improvement in their symptoms after adopting a gluten-free diet. Their condition is called unresponsive or refractory coeliac disease and requires treatment with a gluten-free diet and certain medications.

However, the most common reason for a poor response is that small amounts of gluten are still being eaten. Unless you become skilled at reading food labels, you may inadvertently choose gluten-containing foods when shopping.

Advice from an experienced dietitian is essential for helping you achieve a gluten-free diet that also meets your other nutritional needs. Your local coeliac organization can refer you to an expert dietitian in your area. You may need to see a dietitian frequently during the first few months after you've been diagnosed, but once you've begun mastering your new diet, you'll be able to see them less often. After that, it's still worth consulting your dietitian every 6–12 months (or more often if you still have symptoms or other nutrition-related problems) for a dietary check-up.

**Common symptoms of coeliac disease include:**

- excessive gas (flatulence), abdominal pain and bloating
- chronic diarrhoea; pale, foul-smelling or fatty stools
- nausea, vomiting
- weight loss
- fatigue, headaches, irritability, depression
- anaemia (due to iron or folate deficiency)
- bone or joint pain; muscle cramps
- weakened bones (osteopaenia and osteoporosis) and teeth (loss of tooth enamel and colour)
- menstrual and pregnancy problems in women (missed periods; recurrent miscarriage)
- infertility in men and women
- delayed or stunted growth in infants and children
- pale sores inside the mouth, called aphthous ulcers
- itchy skin rash (dermatitis herpetiformis, DH)

A really important tool for maintaining a gluten-free diet is thoroughly reading the information on food labels.

# Shopping

## Following a gluten-free diet

Maintaining a gluten-free diet means strictly avoiding foods that contain wheat (including spelt, triticale and kamut), rye, barley and ingredients derived from these grains. (Some people with coeliac disease can safely eat oats even though they contain gluten, as long as there are absolutely no traces of other gluten-containing foods present. Be very cautious though; talk to your doctor or dietitian before taking that step).

Although this rules out a lot of foods, such as many types of bread, breakfast cereals, biscuits and pasta, there are many gluten-free versions of these foods available at supermarkets, health-food stores and from specialist food companies.

In addition to gluten-free processed foods, there are also plenty of naturally gluten-free foods available, such as fruit, vegetables, legumes, meat, fish, eggs and nuts. So, it's definitely possible to have a nutritious, balanced gluten-free diet.

Rather than thinking about all of the foods you can't have, focus on enjoying all of the foods you can eat. Some people find that the diagnosis of coeliac disease makes them improve the quality of their diet and their cooking skills, because they no longer rely on processed foods. It's also a great incentive to explore the huge variety of foods available, many of which you may never have eaten before, such as quinoa and buckwheat.

### Become a gluten detective

A really important tool for maintaining a gluten-free diet is thoroughly reading the information on food labels.

Gluten-containing ingredients are present in many processed foods and different brands of the same product can vary in their gluten content (for example, one brand of fish sauce may contain gluten, while another brand doesn't).

A qualified dietitian can help you learn how to interpret the information on food labels, and your local coeliac organization can provide you with information about gluten-free products and ingredients available in your area.

After a while, scanning food labels will become second nature to you and less time-consuming, but initially you may need to take a list or handbook shopping with you.

Many food companies also have lists or information about their gluten-free products available on their websites or from their consumer service departments (contact numbers are often listed on food labels and on websites).

Some companies refrain from adding a gluten-free label to a product, even if it really is gluten-free, because the product may not be gluten-free in the future if they decide to change the ingredients.

Recent improvements to the food labelling laws in some countries have made it much easier for people to find gluten-free foods. All ingredients derived from gluten-containing grains must be declared in the ingredient list on food labels (for example, manufacturers have to list wheat starch rather than just starch), and in some cases a list of the most common allergens that are present must also be provided. Products that have the words 'gluten-free' on their packaging must not contain any detectable gluten, oats or malt. There is also a crossed grain symbol that appears on some gluten-free foods in various countries to let you know that the product has been confirmed to be gluten-free. However, not all gluten-free foods carry this symbol and the food labelling laws differ between various countries.

When possible, always choose a product that has the words 'gluten-free' written on the label. Some products that you would expect to be free of gluten, such as biscuits (cookies) made from rice flour, may be produced in a factory that also makes gluten-containing foods, such as biscuits made from wheat flour. Unless the manufacturer uses separate equipment to make the products and stores the ingredients separately, it is possible for cross-contamination to occur (for example, some gluten-containing wheat flour may end up in the rice flour biscuit).

Some specialist food companies are well aware of the potential for cross-contamination and maintain very strict manufacturing conditions to ensure that their gluten-free products are exactly that. However, not all companies are so aware of the problems of cross-contamination.

It's also important to remember that 'wheat-free' products may not necessarily be free of gluten, so always check the ingredient list for any sources of gluten before purchasing wheat-free foods.

## Sources of gluten

**Major sources**  barley (barley flour, flakes, pearl barley), beer (including ale and lager), couscous, graham flour, kamut, rye (rye flour, flakes), semolina, spelt (dinkel, faro), triticale (triticale flour, flakes), wheat (atta, burghul/bulgar, bran, chapatti flour, flour, germ, einkorn, emmer, farina, hydrolyzed wheat protein, meal, modified wheat starch), and foods based on wheat flour or flaked or puffed wheat (e.g. durum wheat pasta, noodles, cookies, bread, breakfast cereals, cakes, crackers, crumpets, communion wafers, matzoh, muffins, rusks, scones, seitan, sauces)

**Minor sources**  brewer's yeast, cornflour (cornstarch), dextrin (sometimes used in postage stamp adhesive), malt, malted drink powders, malt extract, malt or grain vinegar, maltodextrin, modified starch, oats (bran, gum, flour, pilcorn, rolled, meal, scotch), pre-gel starch, starch, wheat starch, wheaten cornflour (cornstarch), some wheat-starch based thickeners

**Gluten-free options**  amaranth, arrowroot, baking soda, besan (chickpea flour), buckwheat, buckwheat flour, cassava, cassava flour (manioc flour), corn/maize, cornmeal (polenta), cream of tartar, dahl, gelatin, gluten-free flour mixes, gums (acacia, carob bean, carrageenan, guar, xanthum etc), invert sugar, kudzu, legumes, lentil flour, linseed (flax), lotus root flour, lupin, maize cornflour (cornstarch – if free of added wheat flour/starch), maltol, maltose, mannitol, millet, modified maize starch, molasses, potatoes, potato flour, potato starch, psyllium, quinoa, rice, rice bran, rice flour, baby rice cereal, sago, sorghum, soy flour, tapioca, tapioca flour, teff, vinegar (balsamic or wine), yeast

**Food ingredients with no detectable gluten\***  caramel colour, dextrose, glucose, glucose powder, glucose syrup, wheat glucose syrup, wheat-based maltodextrin
\* Even if derived from wheat.

# Products that may contain gluten – always check the ingredient list

- baked beans
- baking powder
- cake icing (frosting)
- cheese, cheese flavouring, cheese sauces and spreads
- chutney
- coffee whitener
- communion wafers
- compound chocolate
- confectionery
- cooking sprays
- corn tortillas
- cornflakes
- croutons
- crumbing mixes
- curry sauces, mixes and powder
- dill pickles and gherkins
- drink mixes
- dry-roasted or seasoned nuts
- energy bars
- flavoured coffees and teas
- flavoured potato chips (crisps)
- frozen chips (fries)
- grated cheese (pre-grated)
- gravy mixes and thickeners
- instant dried mashed potato
- lecithin
- mayonnaise
- meat and seafood substitutes (e.g. vegetable burgers, imitation meats)
- medicines and health supplements (e.g. vitamins, herbal medicines)
- multi-grain or flavoured rice or corn cakes
- mustard
- pickles
- poppadoms
- processed meats (e.g. deli meats, bacon, hot dogs)
- puffed corn cereal and corn cakes
- puffed rice cereal and rice cakes (mixed grain varieties are also available)
- relish
- rice crackers
- rice syrup
- salad dressings
- sauce mixes and marinades
- sauces (e.g. fish, hoisin, oyster, pasta, tomato, soy, sichuan, tamari, worcestershire)
- sausages
- seasoned or flavoured rice mixes
- seasoning and stuffing mixes
- soba noodles
- soft drinks
- soup (fresh, tinned and dried)
- soy milk and soy yoghurt
- stock (ready-made, cubes or powder)
- white pepper (flour may be added for extra bulk)
- yeast
- yoghurt and frozen yoghurt

# Recommended foods* (or gluten-free versions)

## Cereal Products (grains, flours)

- Gluten-free bread, pasta, and breakfast cereals
- Porridge made from soy or rice flakes
- Gluten-free snack bars
- Noodles—rice, mung bean, buckwheat
- Puffed rice and corn cakes
- Gluten-free rice crackers and biscuits
- Rice, millet, quinoa, buckwheat, sorghum, teff, cornmeal (cornstarch), sago, tapioca, rice bran, baby rice cereal
- Gluten-free corn tortillas and taco shells
- Rice paper, gluten-free lasagne or rice noodle sheets

## Fruit and Vegetables

- Fresh fruit and fruit juices
- Dried fruit and glacé fruit
- Fresh vegetables and fresh vegetable juice
- Plain vegetables—frozen, dried, tinned and bottled

## Legumes

- Dried legumes (soaked and freshly boiled)
- Plain, tinned legumes
- Legume flours (e.g. chickpea flour, lentil flour)

## Dairy products and alternatives

- Cow's milk
- Cream, butter, sour cream
- Condensed milk
- Coconut milk
- Gluten-free yoghurts and fromage frais
- Aged cheese and soft cheese
- Gluten-free soy milk (no malt or maltodextrin)
- Plain ice cream
- Tofu
- Rice milk

## Beverages

- Water—tap, spring, mineral, soda, tonic
- Tea, coffee
- Soft drinks
- Fruit juice
- Wine, liqueurs, spirits
- Carob powder and pure unsweetened cocoa powder

## Spreads and condiments

- Jam and pure fruit spreads
- Honey, golden syrup, maple syrup
- Peanut butter
- Vinegar—balsamic and wine
- Lemon juice, lime juice
- Gluten-free tamari
- Tomato paste and purée
- Tahini

# Foods to avoid*

## Cereal Products (grains, flours)

- Bread containing wheat, rye, triticale, oats or barley (or any other gluten-containing ingredient)
- Muesli or breakfast cereals with gluten-containing grains, malt flavourings or malt extract
- Muesli bars, snack bars
- Durum wheat pasta and wheat flour noodles (e.g. instant, udon, hokkien)
- Rolled oats, oat-based porridge, oat bran, oat meal
- Wheat bran, wheat germ, wheat meal
- Couscous
- Semolina

## Fruit and Vegetables

- Some commercial fruit pie fillings
- Some snack foods with fruit fillings
- Battered vegetables and fritters
- Some brands of frozen French fries/chips
- Textured vegetable protein
- Tinned vegetables in sauce

## Legumes

- Tinned baked beans
- Convenience vegetarian meals

## Dairy products and alternatives

- Malted milk and some flavoured milk
- Cheese spreads
- Ice cream in a cone
- Custard and custard powder
- Flavoured ice cream
- Some flavoured yoghurts and dairy desserts

## Beverages

- Drinking chocolate and drink mixes
- Coffee substitutes
- Lemon barley water
- Malted milk drinks
- Beer, lager, ale, stout, Guinness

## Spreads and condiments

- Yeast extract spreads – vegemite, marmite, promite
- Soy sauce
- Commercial chutneys, relishes and pickles
- Malt vinegar
- Commercial salad dressings and mayonnaise
- Many commercial sauces; different brands of the same sauce may vary in their gluten content

* Check all ingredient lists. Individual brands may vary in their gluten content.

# Products to include in a gluten-free kitchen

## Pantry

- gluten-free flours: white rice, potato, chickpea, tapioca (store in opaque containers)
- commercial gluten-free flour mixtures: plain/all-purpose, self-raising, bread mix
- grains: arrowroot, polenta, quinoa, buckwheat, rice, wild rice, sago, tapioca
- gluten-free processed foods: bread, breakfast cereals, biscuits, snack bars and pasta
- noodles: dried rice noodles, mung bean noodles
- nuts and seeds: linseeds (flax seeds), pepitas (pumpkin seeds), sunflower seeds, sesame seeds and raw nuts
- dried legumes and gluten-free tinned varieties: chickpeas, cannellini beans, kidney beans, lentils and split peas
- fruit: gluten-free dried fruit and tinned fruit
- drinks: coffee and tea
- baking ingredients: gluten-free baking powder, baking soda, pure spices, gelatine, natural vanilla extract, xanthan gum, guar gum and psyllium fibre
- sweeteners: sugar, pure icing (confectioners') sugar, pure unsweetened cocoa powder, carob powder
- milk products: UHT milk, condensed milk, dried milk powder, tinned coconut milk
- oils: extra virgin olive oil, olive oil, canola oil, nut oils
- snacks: gluten-free taco shells, plain popping corn, plain gluten-free poppadoms
- tinned fish
- gluten-free sauces: tamari, fish, soy, tomato and pasta

## Refrigerator

- milk: cow's, goat's, gluten-free rice or soy milk
- fats: butter or margarine
- eggs
- dairy products: gluten-free cheese, yoghurt, fromage frais and sour cream
- spreads: pure fruit jam, peanut butter, honey and tahini
- drinks: fruit juice, mineral water and spring water
- corn tortillas
- meat: low-fat gluten-free processed meats and bacon slices
- seeds and flours: ground linseeds (flax seeds), soy flour and brown rice flour (these keep for longer when stored in the refrigerator)
- fruit and vegetables

## Freezer

- gluten-free bread products: bread and breadcrumbs (fresh and dry)
- gluten-free baked goods: muffins and corn tortillas
- stock: home-made gluten-free stock and meals (freeze single portions to reheat when you're too busy to cook)
- gluten-free low-fat ice cream and frozen yoghurt
- gluten-free yeast (this keeps better in the freezer)
- frozen vegetables: spinach, peas, corn, broccoli, cauliflower and stir-fry mixtures

# Cooking

## Ways to a balanced, nutritious gluten-free diet

General healthy eating guidelines for people with coeliac disease, DH and gluten intolerance are the same as those for people without these conditions—with the exception that all foods must be gluten-free and any nutrient deficiencies present after diagnosis need to be corrected through the sensible use of supplements together with healthy eating (supplement use should be guided by your doctor and dietitian):

1  **Eat a wide variety of nutritious foods each day**

   Most of the food you eat each day should be fruit, vegetables (including fresh herbs), legumes and gluten-free cereal products, such as rice and other gluten-free grains, gluten-free bread, pasta and breakfast cereals. If you also have diabetes, you should choose low-GI versions of these foods, such as basmati rice, wild rice, quinoa, corn, sweet potato and temperate fruit. Try to eat a variety of different coloured fruits and vegetables every day. Green vegetables and fresh herbs are excellent sources of folate and various antioxidants, and should be eaten daily.

2  **Watch your fat intake**

   When the villi recover, the intestine is able to absorb more nutrients and some people will start to gain weight. This may be desirable for children and adults who have lost weight, but it's important to keep your weight within the healthy weight range.

   If you need to control your weight, it's important that you don't eat more fat than you need. You can do this by switching to lower-fat dairy products, choosing lean cuts of meat and skinless poultry, using low-fat cooking methods, and minimizing your intake of fatty foods and added fats, such as mayonnaise, oily salad dressings, butter, cream and margarine. Avoid 'junk' foods, and instead snack on nutritious foods, as these will help replenish your body's nutrient stores. For example, choose fresh fruit or cheese on gluten-free bread

Good sources of monounsaturated fat include avocados, olives, olive oil (preferably extra virgin), canola oil and most nuts. Good sources of omega-3 polyunsaturated fat include oily fish (such as salmon, tuna, mackerel, trout, sardines, herrings, blue eye and redfish), omega-3-enriched eggs, walnuts, linseeds (flax seeds) and canola oil. Aim to include fish in your diet 3–4 times a week. The main oils you cook with should be olive and canola oil, and if you eat margarine or mayonnaise, use a variety based on olive or canola oil.

instead of potato chips (crisps) or confectionery.

Improve the quality of fat in your diet by making monounsaturated and omega-3 polyunsaturated fats the main fats in your diet. Unlike saturated fats, these oils help protect against heart disease and Type 2 diabetes. Increasing your omega-3 fat intake can also help reduce inflammation, which may in turn help your villi heal faster.

### 3   Eat moderate amounts of protein-rich foods

Red meat, poultry, eggs, fish and seafood all provide good amounts of protein, iron, zinc and vitamin B12. If you have had undiagnosed coeliac disease for some time, you may not have been absorbing adequate amounts of these important nutrients. Ask your doctor to perform a blood test to check whether you are deficient in iron, folate or vitamin B12. You may initially require nutritional supplements to build up your body's stores, particularly if you're vegetarian.

Try to include rich sources of these nutrients in your diet on a regular basis (for example, red meat at least 3–4 times a week).

Vegetarian sources of protein (such as legumes, tofu and grain-based foods) don't provide as much iron or zinc as animal foods, so if you're vegetarian, it's important to consult a dietitian for advice on how to maximize the amount of iron and zinc you absorb from your meals.

### 4   Regularly eat good sources of calcium

Including calcium-rich foods in your daily diet is essential for reducing the risk of osteoporosis. Dairy foods are the best sources of calcium available because lactose (milk sugar) enhances the body's calcium absorption. Three serves of dairy products a day generally meet most people's calcium requirements (a cup of milk; 200 g (7 oz) yoghurt; a wedge of cheese). However, some people with undiagnosed or newly diagnosed coeliac disease will also be lactose intolerant due to their damaged small intestine, so should choose alternatives such as lactose-free cow's milk and gluten-free soy milk fortified with extra calcium.

People who've had long-standing untreated coeliac disease and/or a low calcium intake may also require a calcium supplement to help boost their body's stores and reduce their risk of osteoporosis as they get older. Ask your doctor or dietitian for advice about whether a calcium supplement is suitable for you. Incorporating regular weight-bearing and strength-building exercises into your lifestyle will also support your bone health.

**5  Include good sources of fibre in your daily diet**

Relying on commercial gluten-free breads, pasta, biscuits and cereals can decrease your fibre intake, because many of these commercial varieties are based on corn and rice flour, which contain less fibre than wheat flour. Fibre-rich foods are important for preventing constipation and other bowel problems.

Good gluten-free sources of fibre include linseed (flax) meal (you can add this to breakfast cereal, yoghurt or baked goods), sunflower seeds (these can be added to salads), brown rice, buckwheat, quinoa, legumes, nuts and fresh vegetables and fruit. If you need more roughage, psyllium husks are a high-fibre gluten-free food that you can add to your diet. And remember to drink water throughout the day—this also helps keep you regular.

**6  Drink gluten-free alcohol in moderation**

If you drink alcohol, enjoy it in moderation. This means consuming no more than two standard drinks on any one day, plus having two or more alcohol-free days each week. In fact, it may be helpful to avoid alcohol entirely during the first few months after being diagnosed with coeliac disease in order to help your gut heal and absorb nutrients properly.

Wine, spirits and liqueurs are typically gluten-free. Beer, stout, ale, Guinness and lager should all be avoided because they contain gluten, however your local coeliac disease support association may be able to advise you of specialist gluten-free brewers.

Stir-fries are a great way to include meat, poultry, fish or seafood in your diet together with a variety of vegetables, and are delicious served with rice or gluten-free rice noodles.

# The challenges of gluten-free baking

Fortunately, many people have been experimenting with gluten-free baking methods for some time, so you can benefit from the results of their experiments.

## Tips For Successful Gluten-Free Baking

○ In baking, a mixture of flours works best, so many commercial gluten-free flour mixtures contain a number of different flours.

○ It's helpful to add some guar gum, xanthan gum or gluten-free pre-gel starch to gluten-free flour mixtures because they mimic the properties of gluten and help reduce crumbling in baked goods. You can get these gums from health-food stores, specialist food stores and some coeliac organizations. For cakes, add 1/4 teaspoon gum per 150 g (51/2 oz/1 cup) of gluten-free flour; for breads, add 1 teaspoon gum per 150 g (51/2 oz/1 cup) of flour; for pizza crusts, add 2 teaspoons gum per 150 g (51/2 oz/1 cup) of flour. Gluten-free gluten substitute is another new ingredient that you can experiment with.

○ You can make your own gluten-free flour mixture and gluten-free baking powder. Sift the flours together three times before using, then substitute by weight, not by volume, when converting recipes.

○ If you find the taste of regular soy flour a little unpleasant, use debittered soy flour.

○ You may achieve better results by increasing the amount of baking powder in cake mixes and by adding an additional egg to gluten-free pancake batters.

○ Gluten-free pastry or biscuit (cookie) dough is easier to work with if you refrigerate it for 30 minutes before forming it into biscuits.

○ Apple sauce can be used instead of oil to add extra moisture to gluten-free waffles, cakes and pancakes without also adding extra fat (although you may need to experiment the first few times).

○ Adding extra eggs, milk powder or soy flour can help to produce a less crumbly texture in gluten-free breads and cakes.

○ Gluten-free bread dough often has a batter-like consistency, and can't be kneaded and shaped as easily as wheat-based

Gluten provides the strength and elasticity that helps hold bakery products together. It also helps baked products rise and gives them a light aerated texture on the inside and a crumbed texture on the surface. Consequently, gluten-free flours don't always produce the same results as wheat flour.

bread dough. However, you can easily make gluten-free bread rolls by using pie tins or muffin tins, or you can shape moulds out of aluminium foil and place them on a baking tray.

- To avoid cross-contamination, make sure you store gluten-free flours separately from gluten-containing flours, in labelled containers. Brown rice flour and soy flour should be stored in the refrigerator, and other gluten-free flours can be stored in a cool dark place. For long-term storage, keep gluten-free flours in the freezer in well-sealed containers. Gluten-free yeast should also be stored in the freezer.

- Gluten-free bakery products may not keep their freshness as long as regular versions, but you can wrap and freeze individual portions of gluten-free bakery goods so you can enjoy them later.

- Using heavy-duty tins for baking, rather than aluminium ones, will help gluten-free cakes and breads cook evenly so that the centre is cooked at the same time as the outside, rather than having a soggy centre and a hard crust. Test your tins with a magnet—if the magnet sticks to the tin, it's fine to use. Ring-shaped tins are particularly good for cakes. To prevent the dough from sticking to the tin, grease the cooking tin or line it with baking paper before adding the dough.

- To produce a good gluten-free bakery product, you need the right ingredients and the right oven temperature. Sometimes gluten-free baked goods don't work because the oven isn't working properly. Check it with an oven thermometer, which can be purchased from a good kitchenware shop or over the internet.

- Make your own gluten-free dried breadcrumbs by placing gluten-free bread slices in a slow oven to dry (the bread should turn a golden colour), then put the dried bread in a food processor or crush it with a rolling pin. The breadcrumbs can be stored in the freezer for several months.

- Commercial gluten-free bread mixes can be used to make pizza bases (don't let the dough rise), pikelets and pancakes.

- Remember that no matter how much you experiment, some bakery products just won't work when made with gluten-free flour. However, there are plenty of other delicious gluten-free recipes you can try instead.

Gluten-free breads can sink after being taken out of an oven if the kitchen is too humid or if the bread was left to rise for too long before being placed in the oven. If you make a yeast-leavened dough that doesn't rise properly, make it again and add a teaspoon of vinegar or a pinch of citric acid to the water before you add the yeast.

## Make your own flour mixes

### Plain (all-purpose) flour
**1**  Mix 6 parts rice flour with 2 parts potato flour and 1 part tapioca flour.

**2**  Mix 2 parts soy flour with 1 part rice flour and 1 part potato flour.

**3**  Use 1 part each of soy flour and potato flour; soy flour and rice flour; or soy flour and maize cornflour (cornstarch).

**4**  Use 4 parts soy flour, 4 parts potato flour, 1 part rice flour, and 1 part glutinous rice flour.

### Self-raising flour
Put 2 tablespoons potato flour into a measuring cup, then add sufficient white rice flour to bring the total volume of the mixture to 1 cup. Sift the mixture into a bowl and add ½ teaspoon bicarbonate of soda (baking soda), ½ teaspoon cream of tartar, and 1 teaspoon xanthan gum (or guar gum).

### Baking powder
Mix together 1 part bicarbonate of soda (baking soda) and 2 parts cream of tartar.

## Eating well with gluten intolerance

- Keep your pantry, refrigerator and freezer well stocked with gluten-free foods, so you always have something suitable on hand when you need it.
- If you have a busy lifestyle, cook double portions of meals, so you can freeze the leftovers.
- Take suitable foods with you to work, school, the movies, social events and while shopping or travelling.
- Contact your local coeliac organization to find out about restaurants and cafés in your area that cater for people on gluten-free diets.
- If you're in doubt about a menu item, ask the waiter or chef about the ingredients and preparation methods or ask if a gluten-free option is available.
- If some people in your family eat regular foods and others require gluten-free foods, make sure you store the two types of foods separately to avoid cross-contamination.
- You may need to designate a special shelf in the pantry as being for gluten-free foods only to ensure gluten-containing

If some people in your family eat regular foods and others require gluten-free foods, make sure you store the two types of foods separately to avoid cross-contamination.

foods are not grabbed by mistake. Use separate cutting boards and knives and use separate toasters (or shake out the crumbs thoroughly before toasting gluten-free bread) to make sure that gluten-free bread is not contaminated. You may also need to have separate containers of margarine, butter and spreads, so gluten-containing breadcrumbs are not eaten by family members who need to follow a gluten-free diet.

○ If your child requires a gluten-free diet, speak with their teachers and the parents of their friends about their condition and dietary requirements. You may like to offer to send some gluten-free treats along to any parties or social events they attend.

## Disclaimer

All the recipes in this book are free of gluten. For ingredients that typically contain gluten (such as flour, bread and cereals) we have specified that you choose a gluten-free version. For ingredients that occasionally contain gluten we have used the symbol **GF** so you know to check the ingredient list.

The nutritional analysis of recipes does not include any serving suggestions or garnishes.

The information in this book is intended for people with coeliac disease, dermatitis herpetiformis (DH) and or gluten/wheat intolerance, and people who care for them. It contains general advice about healthy gluten-free eating. This advice may not be sufficient for some people with multiple health problems or serious complications. It is not intended to replace any advice given to you by a qualified doctor or other mainstream health professional. It is important that coeliac disease, DH and dietary intolerances are diagnosed by a doctor, using standard diagnostic tests (blood samples, biopsies and assessment of your symptoms). Neither the author nor the publishers can be held responsible for claims arising from the inappropriate use or incorrect interpretation of any of the dietary advice described in this book.

# Breakfast

**nutrition per serve (6)**  Energy **315 kJ (75 Cal)**  Fat **0.3 g**  Saturated fat **0 g**
Protein **2 g**  Carbohydrate **15.6 g**  Fibre **2.8 g**  Cholesterol **0 mg**  Sodium **6 g**

# Citrus summer salad

**3 ruby grapefruit**

**3 large oranges**

**1 tbsp caster (superfine) sugar**

**1 cinnamon stick**

**1 tbsp mint, chopped**

**whole mint leaves, to garnish**

**low-fat plain yoghurt, to serve**

**Prep time** 15 minutes

**Cooking time** 5 minutes

**Serves** 4–6

**1**  Peel and remove the pith from the grapefruit and oranges. Carefully cut out the segments and mix together in a bowl.

**2**  Put the sugar, cinnamon stick and mint in a small saucepan with 3 tablespoons water and stir over low heat until the sugar has dissolved.

**3**  Remove the cinnamon stick and strain the mint from the syrup, then drizzle the syrup over the fruit. Garnish with fresh mint leaves and serve with yoghurt.

nutrition per serve   Energy **1293 kJ (309 Cal)** Fat **12.5 g** Saturated fat **5.3 g**
Protein **7.2 g** Carbohydrate **40 g** Fibre **2.5 g** Cholesterol **82 mg** Sodium **700 g**

# Waffles

**250 g (9 oz/2 cups) soy-containing, gluten-free self-raising flour**

**3 tbsp caster (superfine) sugar**

**300 ml (10½ fl oz) milk**

**2 eggs**

**60 g (2¼ oz) butter, melted, cooled butter, to serve**

**strawberry jam** <sup>GF</sup> **(Basics), to serve**

**Prep time** 10 minutes +
15 minutes resting
**Cooking time** 30 minutes
**Makes** 6

**1** To make the batter, sift the flour into a large bowl, stir in the sugar, then make a well in the centre. In a separate bowl, whisk the milk and eggs together. Pour the milk mixture into the well in the dry ingredients and whisk until smooth. Whisk in the melted butter. Set the batter aside to rest for 10–15 minutes.

**2** Preheat a waffle maker. Pour ⅓-cupfuls (4 tablespoons) of the batter into the waffle maker and cook following the waffle maker's instructions. Transfer to a wire rack and repeat with the remaining batter, allowing the waffle maker to reheat between waffles. Serve the waffles with strawberry jam.

## nutrition per serve   Energy **2303 kJ (550 Cal)**  Fat **29.3 g**  Saturated fat **6.8 g**
Protein **30.5 g**  Carbohydrate **41.4 g**  Fibre **7.1 g**  Cholesterol **563 mg**  Sodium **560 g**

# Scrambled eggs with tomatoes

4 field mushrooms

2 vine-ripened tomatoes, halved

canola or olive oil spray

2 tsp thyme, plus extra to garnish

6 eggs

1 tbsp reduced-fat milk

30 g (1 oz) reduced-fat canola or olive oil margarine

4 slices of gluten-free bread, toasted

1   Put the mushrooms and tomatoes, cut side up, under a preheated grill (broiler), then spray with oil and scatter with the thyme leaves. Cook for 3–5 minutes, or until warmed.

2   Meanwhile, break the eggs into a bowl, add the milk and season well with salt and freshly ground black pepper. Whisk gently with a fork until well combined.

3   Melt half the margarine in a small non-stick saucepan or frying pan over low heat. Add the eggs, then stir constantly with a wooden spoon. Do not turn up the heat—scrambling must be done slowly and gently. When most of the egg has set, add the remaining margarine and remove the pan from the heat. There should be enough heat left in the pan to finish cooking the eggs and melt the margarine. Serve immediately on toast. Arrange the tomatoes and mushrooms on the side. Garnish with extra thyme leaves.

**Prep time** 5 minutes
**Cooking time** 10 minutes
**Serves** 2

nutrition per serve   Energy **1772 kJ (422 Cal)** Fat **16.1 g** Saturated fat **5.4 g**
Protein **26.1 g** Carbohydrate **42.5 g** Fibre **8.3 g** Cholesterol **386 mg** Sodium **497 g**

# Poached eggs with spinach

**Dressing**

**125 g (4½ oz/½ cup) low-fat
  plain yoghurt**

**1 small garlic clove, crushed**

**1 tbsp snipped chives**

**300 g (10½ oz/6 cups) baby
  English spinach leaves**

**15 g (½ oz) butter**

**4 tomatoes, halved**

**1 tbsp white vinegar**

**8 eggs**

**8 thick slices of gluten-free bread,
  toasted**

**Prep time** 10 minutes
**Cooking time** 15 minutes
**Serves 4**

**1** To make the dressing, mix together the yoghurt, garlic and chives.

**2** Wash the spinach and put it in a large saucepan with just the little water that is left clinging to the leaves. Cover the pan and cook over low heat for 3–4 minutes, or until the spinach has wilted. Add the butter, then season with salt and freshly ground black pepper and toss together. Remove pan from heat and keep warm.

**3** Put the tomatoes, cut side up, under a preheated grill (broiler) and cook for 3–5 minutes, or until softened and warm.

**4** Fill a deep frying pan three-quarters full with cold water and add the vinegar and some salt to stop the egg whites spreading. Bring the water to a gentle simmer. Gently break an egg into a small bowl, then carefully slide the egg into the water, then repeat with remaining eggs. Reduce the heat so that the water barely moves. Cook for 1–2 minutes, or until the eggs are just set. Remove with a spatula. Drain on paper towels.

**5** Top each slice of toast with some spinach, an egg and some dressing. Serve with the grilled tomato halves on the side.

nutrition per serve   Energy **1509 kJ (361 Cal)** Fat **21.8 g** Saturated fat **2.4 g**
Protein **8.9 g** Carbohydrate **25.9 g** Fibre **9.5 g** Cholesterol **0 mg** Sodium **9 g**

# Wheat-free muesli

90 g (3¼ oz/3 cups) gluten-free puffed corn (non-malted)

60 g (2¼ oz/2 cups) puffed rice ᴳᶠ

90 g (3¼ oz/1 cup) rice bran

100 g (3½ oz/1 cup) LSA mix

80 g (2¾ oz/½ cup) roasted unsalted macadamia nuts, chopped

70 g (2½ oz/½ cup) roasted hazelnuts, chopped

70 g (2½ oz/½ cup) pepitas (pumpkin seeds)

60 g (2¼ oz/½ cup) sunflower seeds

135 g (4¾ oz/1 cup) chopped mixed dried fruit, such as dried pears, peaches and apricots

fruit juice or milk, to serve

low-fat plain yoghurt, to serve

**Prep time** 10 minutes
**Cooking time** Nil
**Serves** 10

**1**  Put the grains, nuts, seeds and dried fruit in a large bowl and stir together thoroughly. Store in an airtight container until ready to use.

**2**  When ready to serve, top with the fruit juice or milk and the yoghurt.

# Buckwheat pancakes

**135 g (4¾ oz/1 cup) buckwheat flour**

**1 egg**

**pure maple syrup, to serve**

**Prep time** 10 minutes
**Cooking time** 20 minutes
**Makes** 16–20

**1**  Sift the flour into a bowl and make a well in the centre. In a separate bowl mix the egg with 185 ml (6 fl oz/ ¾ cup) water, then pour into the well in the dry ingredients. Beat with a wooden spoon until the batter is combined and smooth. Pour the batter into a vessel with a pouring lip.

**2**  Brush a 20 cm (8 in) frying pan with oil and heat over medium heat. Pour in just enough batter to thinly cover the bottom of the pan.

**3**  When the top of the pancake starts to set, turn it over with a spatula. After browning the second side, transfer to a plate. Repeat with the remaining pancake batter, greasing the pan between batches. Serve with a drizzle of maple syrup.

nutrition per serve  Energy **1423 kJ (340 Cal)** Fat **14.2 g** Saturated fat **4.4 g**
Protein **26.6 g** Carbohydrate **25.3 g** Fibre **2.3 g** Cholesterol **384 mg** Sodium **422g**

# Herb omelette with tomatoes

**250 g (9 oz) red or yellow cherry tomatoes, halved**

**4 eggs, lightly beaten**

**1 handful chopped mixed herbs (e.g. parsley, chives, oregano)**

**2 egg whites**

**3 tbsp grated low-fat cheddar cheese** <sup>GF</sup>

**1 handful baby rocket (arugula) leaves**

**2 slices of gluten-free bread, toasted**

**Prep time** 15 minutes
**Cooking time** 20 minutes
**Serves** 2

1  Preheat the oven to 180°C (350°F/Gas 4). Line a baking tray with baking paper. Place tomatoes, cut side up, on prepared tray. Season well with salt and freshly ground black pepper. Bake for 15 minutes, or until softened. Reserve about one-third of tomatoes for garnish.

2  Whisk together the whole eggs and mixed herbs in a bowl. Beat the egg whites in a small bowl with electric beaters until soft peaks form. Gently whisk the egg whites into the egg and herb mixture.

3  Preheat a grill (broiler) to medium heat. Heat a 22 cm (8½ in) omelette pan or frying pan and lightly brush with oil. Pour in half of the egg mixture and leave for 1–2 minutes, or until lightly browned underneath.

4  Scatter half the cheese over the egg mixture and place the pan under the grill for 1 minute, or until the egg is set and the cheese is melted. Top with half of the remaining tomatoes and half of the rocket. Fold the omelette in half and carefully slide from the pan onto a plate. Scatter half the reserved tomatoes over omelette.

5  Gently re-whisk the remaining egg mixture, then cook a second omelette in the same way as the first. Serve with the toast.

nutrition per serve   Energy **1497 kJ (358 Cal)**  Fat **21.7 g**  Saturated fat **3.1 g**
Protein **29.6 g**  Carbohydrate **9.9 g**  Fibre **19.7 g**  Cholesterol **3 mg**  Sodium **239 g**

# Home-made baked beans

**550 g (1 lb 4 oz/3 cups) dried soya
  beans**

**400 g (14 oz) tin diced tomatoes**

**250 ml (9 fl oz/1 cup) vegetable
  stock ᴳᶠ (Basics)**

**1 bay leaf**

**2 tbsp chopped parsley**

**pinch of dried thyme**

**1 tbsp canola or olive oil**

**1**  Cook the soya beans in plenty of water for about
4 hours, or until tender. Drain. Preheat the oven to
180°C (350°F/Gas 4).

**2**  Put the soya beans in a casserole dish and add the
tinned tomatoes, stock, herbs and oil. Bake, covered, for
40 minutes. Check the consistency of the sauce. If you
want a thicker consistency, remove the lid of the
casserole dish and cook for a further 10–15 minutes, or
until reduced to the desired consistency.

**Prep time** 5 minutes

**Cooking time** 4 hours 40 minutes

**Serves** 6

**nutrition per serve**   Energy **845 kJ (202 Cal)**  Fat **2.8 g**  Saturated fat **1.2 g**
Protein **3.7 g**  Carbohydrate **39 g**  Fibre **3.8 g**  Cholesterol **6 mg**  Sodium **1092 g**

# Crumpets

450 g (1 lb/3 cups) gluten-free self-raising flour

1 tbsp caster (superfine) sugar

1 tsp salt

2 tsp dried yeast ᴳᶠ

435 ml (15¼ fl oz/1¾ cups) lukewarm milk

½ tsp bicarbonate of soda (baking soda)

butter, to serve

strawberry jam ᴳᶠ (Basics), to serve

**1**  Combine flour, sugar, salt and yeast in a large bowl. Pour in milk and whisk to combine. Cover and set aside in a warm place for 1 hour, or until doubled in size.

**2**  Use a spoon to beat the mixture until it deflates. Combine  4 tablespoons lukewarm water and bicarbonate of soda in a bowl, then whisk until smooth. Set aside for 15 minutes.

**3**  Brush a large heavy-based non-stick frying pan with oil and heat over medium heat. Brush four 9.5 x 2 cm (3¾ x ¾ in) crumpet rings with oil, then place in pan and reduce heat to low. Pour batter into each crumpet ring to fill three-quarters full. Cook for 12–15 minutes, or until large bubbles come to surface, the base is golden and top is set. Cover the pan and cook for a further 2–3 minutes. Use a sharp knife to carefully loosen crumpets and remove from rings. Put crumpets on a wire rack. Wash crumpet rings and re-grease. Repeat with remaining batter. Serve with butter and fruit jam.

**Prep time** 15 minutes +
1¼ hours standing
**Cooking time** 45 minutes
**Makes** 10

# Pancakes

190 g (6¾ oz/1¼ cups) gluten-free plain (all-purpose) flour
2 tsp gluten-free baking powder
1 egg
1 tbsp canola or olive oil
mixed berries, to serve
pure maple syrup, to serve

**1** Sift flour and baking powder into a bowl and make a well in the centre. Mix together the egg, oil and 310 ml (10¾ fl oz/1¼ cups) water, then add to the well in the dry ingredients. Stir until the batter is smooth and reaches the consistency of thin cream, adding up to another 3 tablespoons water if necessary. Strain the batter into a vessel with a pouring lip.

**2** Lightly brush a 20 cm (8 in) frying pan with oil and heat over medium heat. Pour in just enough mixture to thinly cover the bottom of the pan. When the top of the pancake starts to set, use a spatula to turn it over. After browning the second side, transfer to a plate. Repeat with remaining pancake batter, greasing pan between each batch. Serve with berries and maple syrup.

**Prep time** 10 minutes
**Cooking time** 20 minutes
**Makes** 10

## nutrition per serve (6)   Energy **737 kJ (176 Cal)** Fat **1.8 g** Saturated fat **0.2 g**
Protein **5.1 g** Carbohydrate **32.4 g** Fibre **3.8 g** Cholesterol **0 mg** Sodium **8 g**

# Fresh fruit quinoa

**175 g (6 oz/1 cup) organic quinoa**

**500 ml (17 fl oz/2 cups) unsweetened apple and blackcurrant juice**

**1 cinnamon stick**

**2 tsp grated orange zest**

**2 fresh figs, chopped**

**2 peaches or nectarines**

**200 g (7 oz/1⅓ cups) strawberries, hulled and chopped**

**low-fat plain yoghurt, to serve**

**mint leaves, to garnish**

1   Rinse the quinoa under cold running water and drain. Put the quinoa, juice and cinnamon stick in a saucepan.

2   Bring to the boil, cover and simmer for 10–15 minutes, or until all the liquid has been absorbed and the quinoa is translucent and the spiral germ ring is visible. Remove the cinnamon stick. Cover and set aside to firm up and cool a little.

3   Fold in the orange zest and half of the chopped fruit. Spoon the mixture into four bowls and sprinkle with the remaining fruit. Serve with a generous dollop of the yoghurt. Garnish with fresh mint leaves and serve immediately.

**Prep time** 10 minutes
**Cooking time** 15 minutes
**Serves** 4–6

**nutrition per serve**  Energy **954 kJ (278 Cal)**  Fat **5 g**  Saturated fat **2.5 g**
Protein **21.1 g**  Carbohydrate **25.4 g**  Fibre **1.7 g**  Cholesterol **29 mg**  Sodium **1774 g**

# Italian-style breakfast toasts

4 Roma (plum) tomatoes, halved

2 large field mushrooms, halved

canola or olive oil spray

8 slices of low-fat bacon GF

165 g (5¾ oz/⅔ cup) plain cottage
   cheese

2 tbsp chopped flat-leaf (Italian)
   parsley

1 tbsp snipped chives

4 slices of gluten-free bread, toasted

balsamic vinegar, to drizzle

**1**  Preheat the grill (broiler). Place the tomatoes, cut side
up, and the mushrooms on a large baking tray. Lightly
spray with the oil. Season well with black pepper. Pat
the bacon dry with paper towels and place on the tray.
Grill tomatoes, mushrooms and bacon for 5–8 minutes,
or until cooked. Turn the bacon slices once and remove
them as they cook and become crisp.

**2**  Combine the cottage cheese, parsley and chives. Spread
thickly over the toasted bread. Arrange the tomatoes,
mushrooms and bacon over the top. Drizzle with a little
balsamic vinegar, then serve while hot.

**Prep time** 15 minutes
**Cooking time** 10 minutes
**Serves** 4

nutrition per serve   Energy **1146 kJ (274 Cal)** Fat **13.5 g** Saturated fat **4.4 g**
Protein **10.6 g** Carbohydrate **26.7 g** Fibre **1.6 g** Cholesterol **200 mg** Sodium **211 g**

# Eggs en cocotte

**1 tbsp olive oil**

**1 garlic clove, crushed**

**3 vine-ripened tomatoes (about
300 g/10½ oz), peeled, seeded
and chopped**

**½ tsp olive oil, extra**

**4 eggs**

**2 tbsp snipped chives**

**4 slices of thick gluten-free bread**

**15 g (½ oz) butter**

**Prep time** 15 minutes
**Cooking time** 30 minutes
**Serves** 4

**1**  Preheat the oven to 180°C (350°F/Gas 4). To make the
tomato sauce, heat the oil in a heavy-based frying pan.
Add the garlic and cook for 30 seconds. Add the tomato
and season with salt and freshly ground black pepper.
Cook over medium heat for 15 minutes, or until
thickened.

**2**  Grease four 125 ml (4 fl oz/½ cup) ramekins with the
extra olive oil, then carefully break 1 egg into each,
trying not to break the yolk. Pour the tomato sauce
evenly around the outside of each egg, so the yolk is still
visible. Sprinkle with chives and season lightly with salt
and freshly ground black pepper.

**3**  Place the ramekins in a deep baking dish and pour in
enough hot water to come halfway up the outside of the
ramekins. Bake for about 10–12 minutes, or until the
egg white is set. Toast the bread and lightly spread the
slices with the butter. Serve immediately with the
cooked eggs.

**nutrition per serve** Energy **1239 kJ (295 Cal)** Fat **0.5 g** Saturated fat **0 g**
Protein **3.8 g** Carbohydrate **70.8 g** Fibre **7.9 g** Cholesterol **0 mg** Sodium **42 g**

# Dried fruit compote

400 g (14 oz/3 cups) dried fruit salad mixture (dried
   peaches, prunes, pears, apricots, apples and nectarines)

500 ml (17 fl oz/2 cups) orange juice

1 tsp soft brown sugar

1–2 star anise

1 vanilla bean, halved lengthways

low-fat plain yoghurt, to serve

**1** Put the dried fruit salad mixture in a saucepan. Add the
orange juice, sugar, star anise and vanilla bean. Bring
slowly to the boil, then reduce the heat, cover and leave
to simmer, stirring occasionally, for 15 minutes, or until
the fruit is plump and juicy.

**2** Discard the star anise and vanilla bean. Serve the fruit
drizzled with the cooking syrup. Add a dollop of
yoghurt to serve.

**Prep time** 10 minutes
**Cooking time** 15 minutes
**Serves** 4

# Snacks, light meals and sides

nutrition per serve   Energy **1126 kJ (269 Cal)** Fat **15.8 g** Saturated fat **2.1 g**
Protein **20 g** Carbohydrate **7.9 g** Fibre **12.1 g** Cholesterol **3 mg** Sodium **14 g**

# Puffed corn snack mix

**360 g (12¾ oz/12 cups) gluten-free puffed corn breakfast cereal**

**400 g (14 oz) packet dried fruit and raw nut mixture**

**90 g (3¼ oz/1 cup) rice bran**

**55 g (2 oz/1 cup) flaked coconut, toasted**

**4 tbsp pepitas (pumpkin seeds)**

**260 g (9¼ oz/¾ cup) honey**

**Prep time** 10 minutes

**Cooking time** 20 minutes

**Serves** 20

1  Preheat the oven to 180°C (350°F/Gas 4). Line four baking trays with baking paper. Place the puffed corn, dried fruit and nut mixture, bran, flaked coconut and pepitas in a large bowl and mix together well.

2  Heat the honey in a saucepan over low heat for 3 minutes, or until it thins to a pouring consistency. Pour over the puffed corn mixture and stir until all the dry ingredients are well coated with the honey.

3  Spread the mixture on the lined baking trays in a single layer and bake for 15 minutes, or until golden, turning the cereal several times during cooking. Cool completely before storing in an airtight container in a cool, dark place.

nutrition per serve    Energy **1611 kJ (385 Cal)**  Fat **34.3 g**  Saturated fat **4.5 g**
Protein **12.2 g**  Carbohydrate **5.7 g**  Fibre **5.1 g**  Cholesterol **0 mg**  Sodium **567 g**

# Tamari nut mix

**235 g (8½ oz/1¾ cups) mixed raw unsalted nuts (almonds, Brazil nuts, peanuts, walnuts)**

**110 g (3¾ oz/¾ cup) pepitas (pumpkin seeds)**

**125 g (4½ oz/1 cup) sunflower seeds**

**115 g (4 oz/¾ cup) raw unsalted cashew nuts**

**150 g (5½ oz/scant 1 cup) raw unsalted macadamia nuts**

**125 ml (4 fl oz/½ cup) tamari** GF

**1**  Preheat the oven to 140°C (275°F/Gas 1). You will need two large baking trays.

**2**  Place the mixed nuts, pepitas, sunflower seeds, cashew nuts and macadamia nuts in a large bowl. Pour the tamari over the nuts and seeds, then toss together well, coating them evenly. Set aside for 10 minutes.

**3**  Spread the nut and seed mixture evenly over the baking trays and bake for 20–25 minutes, or until dry-roasted as desired. Cool completely.

**Prep time** 10 minutes +
10 minutes standing
**Cooking time** 25 minutes
**Makes** 750 g (1 lb 10 oz/4 cups)
**Serves** 12

# Eggplant sambal

2 eggplants (aubergines), halved

canola or olive oil spray

½ tsp ground turmeric

3 tbsp lime juice

2 red chillies, seeded and finely chopped

1 red onion, finely chopped

4 tbsp plain yoghurt

**1**  Preheat the oven to 200°C (400°F/Gas 6). Put the eggplants in a roasting tin, cut side up. Spray the cut halves of the eggplants with the oil and sprinkle with the turmeric. Roast for 30 minutes, or until they are browned all over and very soft.

**2**  Scoop the eggplant pulp into a bowl, then mash with the lime juice, chilli and red onion, reserving some chilli and onion for garnish.

**3**  Season with salt, then fold in the yoghurt. Garnish with the remaining onion and chilli.

**Prep time** 15 minutes
**Cooking time** 30 minutes
**Serves** 4

# Hummus

**220 g (7¾ oz/1 cup) dried chickpeas**

**2 tbsp tahini** GF

**4 garlic cloves, crushed**

**4 tbsp lemon juice, plus extra
    (optional)**

**2 tbsp olive oil**

**2 tsp ground cumin**

**large pinch of cayenne pepper**

**½ tsp salt**

**paprika, to sprinkle**

**1 tbsp chopped parsley**

**Prep time** 20 minutes +
overnight soaking
**Cooking time** 1¼ hours
**Serves** 20

**1** Put chickpeas in a large bowl, cover with water and leave to soak overnight. Drain, then rinse well.

**2** Transfer the chickpeas to a large saucepan and cover with cold water. Bring to the boil, then reduce the heat and simmer for 1¼ hours, or until the chickpeas are very tender, occasionally skimming any froth from the surface. Drain well, reserving about 250 ml (9 fl oz/1 cup) of the cooking liquid. Leave the chickpeas until cool enough to handle. Pick over for any loose skins and discard.

**3** Process the chickpeas, tahini, garlic, lemon juice, olive oil, cumin, salt and cayenne pepper in a food processor until thick and smooth. With the motor still running, gradually add about 185 ml (6 fl oz/¾ cup) of the reserved cooking liquid to form a smooth creamy purée. Add extra lemon juice, to taste, if necessary.

**4** Spread onto a flat bowl or plate, sprinkle with paprika and scatter the parsley over the top.

# Mushroom pâté

1 tsp olive oil

1 small onion, chopped

2 garlic cloves, crushed

300 g (10½ oz) flat mushrooms, wiped clean and chopped

4 tbsp dry white wine or water

80 g (2¾ oz/1 cup) fresh gluten-free breadcrumbs

2 tbsp thyme, plus extra to serve

2 tbsp chopped flat-leaf (Italian) parsley

1 tbsp lemon juice

**Prep time** 15 minutes +
1 hour refrigeration
**Cooking time** 10 minutes
**Serves** 4–6

**1**  Heat the oil in a large, deep frying pan. Add the onion and garlic and cook, stirring, for 2 minutes without browning. Add the mushrooms and white wine or water. Cook, stirring for 1 minute, then cover and simmer for 5 minutes, stirring once or twice. Remove the lid and increase heat to evaporate any liquid. Cool.

**2**  Place the mushroom mixture, breadcrumbs, herbs and lemon juice in a food processor. Process until smooth and season well with salt and black pepper. Spoon into a serving bowl. Cover and refrigerate for at least 1 hour to allow the flavours to develop.

nutrition per serve (8)   Energy **1600 kJ (382 Cal)**  Fat **20.6 g**  Saturated fat **5.2 g**
Protein **41.1 g**  Carbohydrate **4.3 g**  Fibre **0.5 g**  Cholesterol **205 mg**  Sodium **1025 g**

# Veal and chicken terrine

**2 tbsp canola or olive oil**

**2 garlic cloves, crushed**

**1 leek, washed and finely chopped**

**1 kg (2 lb 4 oz) minced (ground) veal**

**1 handful snipped chives**

**3 eggs, lightly beaten**

**2 tbsp canola or olive oil, extra**

**3 tbsp gin**

**1½ tsp salt**

**40 g (1½ oz/½ cup) fresh gluten-free
breadcrumbs**

**2 boneless, skinless chicken breasts,
each cut into four long strips**

**Prep time** 45 minutes

**Cooking time** 1½ hours

**Serves** 6–8

**1**  Preheat oven to 180°C (350°F/Gas 4). Grease 20 x 10 cm (8 x 4 in) loaf (bar) tin, then line with foil.

**2**  Heat oil in a frying pan over medium heat, add garlic and leek and fry for about 5 minutes, or until soft. Allow to cool. Transfer to a bowl, then add veal, chives, eggs, extra oil, gin, salt and breadcrumbs. Using your hands, mix and knead mixture until it is well combined.

**3**  Put half of the mince mixture into the prepared tin, pressing down well. Lay the chicken breast strips over the meat. Press the remaining mince mixture over the chicken. Cover with greased foil. Place in a baking dish and add enough boiling water to come halfway up the sides of the loaf tin. Bake for 1¼–1½ hours.

**4**  When cooked, remove loaf tin from the dish of water and drain off any liquid. Put a piece of cardboard on top of the terrine, then weigh it down with a heavy weight (for instance, tins of food). Refrigerate until cold.

# Pumpkin and feta pizza

450 g (1 lb/3 cups) gluten-free plain (all-purpose) flour

4 tsp dried yeast GF

½ tsp sugar

1 tsp salt

1½ tbsp canola or olive oil

**Topping**

**500 g (1 lb 2 oz) pumpkin (winter squash), peeled, seeded and chopped**

**canola or olive oil spray**

**1 tbsp canola or olive oil**

**2 onions, thinly sliced**

**2 garlic cloves, crushed**

**3 tbsp pine nuts**

**3 tbsp tomato paste (concentrated purée) GF**

**1 garlic clove, extra, crushed**

**1 tsp dried oregano**

**125 g (4½ oz) reduced-fat feta cheese, crumbled**

**4 tbsp black olives, pitted and crushed**

**2 tbsp thyme**

**Prep time** 45 minutes +
1 hour rising
**Cooking time** 1 hour 5 minutes
**Serves** 4

**1**  Combine yeast, sugar and 3 tablespoons warm water in a small bowl and set aside until foaming. Sift flour and salt into a large bowl. In a separate bowl mix together 250 ml (9 fl oz/1 cup) warm water and the oil, then pour into the well in dry ingredients along with yeast mixture. Use a wooden spoon to mix until almost combined. Use your hands to mix into a soft dough.

**2**  Lightly dust a board with gluten-free flour. Turn the dough out onto the board and knead until smooth. Place the dough in a lightly oiled bowl. Cover and set aside in a warm place for 1 hour, or until the dough has doubled in size.

**3**  Meanwhile, make topping. Preheat oven to 180°C (350°F/Gas 4). Line a baking tray. Put pumpkin on tray and spray with oil. Bake for 45 minutes. Set aside. Increase oven temperature to 220°C (425°F/Gas 7). While pumpkin is cooking, heat oil in a large non-stick frying pan over medium heat. Add onion and garlic and cook for 5 minutes. Stir in pine nuts, remove from heat and set aside. In a small bowl combine the tomato paste, garlic and oregano with 1 tablespoon water.

**4**  Use your fist to punch dough down, then knead until it returns to its original size. Grease two 27 cm (10¾ in) pizza trays. Divide dough into two portions. On a surface dusted with gluten-free flour, roll out one portion to fit the tray, then place dough onto tray. Repeat with the remaining dough. Spread tomato paste mixture over each pizza base, then spread onion mixture over. Scatter pumpkin, feta, olives and thyme over top. Bake for 20 minutes or until dough is golden.

nutrition per serve   Energy **2311 kJ (552 Cal)** Fat **23.5 g**  Saturated fat **5.8 g**
Protein **62.4 g** Carbohydrate **23.8 g** Fibre **0 g** Cholesterol **267 mg** Sodium **881 g**

# Glazed drumsticks

**8 large chicken drumsticks (skin removed)**

**4 tbsp golden syrup or honey**

**3 tbsp pear juice**

**1 tbsp canola or olive oil**

**1 tsp salt**

**1**  Put the drumsticks in a shallow non-metallic dish.
Combine the remaining ingredients and pour the
marinade over the drumsticks, making sure they are all
coated. Marinate overnight, turning occasionally.

**2**  Preheat the oven to 180°C (350°F/Gas 4). Put the
drumsticks and marinade into a baking dish. Bake for
35–40 minutes, turning frequently during cooking and
brushing with the pan juices. If the pan juices start to
overbrown, add a small amount of water or stock until
syrupy. Serve hot or cold.

**Prep time** 20 minutes +
overnight marinating
**Cooking time** 40 minutes
Serves 4

# Crispy wafer biscuits

**175 g (6 oz/1 cup) rice flour**

**125 g (4½ oz/1 cup) pure maize cornflour (cornstarch)** GF

**40 g (1½ oz/½ cup) rice bran**

**½ tsp salt**

**2 tbsp canola or olive oil**

**Prep time** 10 minutes
**Cooking time** 25 minutes
**Makes** about 40

**1**  Preheat the oven to 200°C (400°F/Gas 6). Lightly grease two 30 x 25 cm (12 x 10 in) Swiss roll (jelly roll) tins.

**2**  Combine the dry ingredients in a bowl and make a well in the middle. In a separate bowl mix together 185 ml (6 fl oz/¾ cup) water and the oil, then pour into the well in the dry ingredients. Mix until thoroughly combined.

**3**  Divide the mixture into two portions. Press each portion of dough into one of the prepared tins and bake for 20–25 minutes. Cool in the tin. Break into pieces and store in an airtight container for up to 2 days.

nutrition per quiche   Energy **579 kJ (138 Cal)**  Fat **7.7 g**  Saturated fat **3.7 g**
Protein **3 g**  Carbohydrate **13.7 g**  Fibre **1.5 g**  Cholesterol **55 mg**  Sodium **340 g**

# Mini potato and leek quiches

**600 g (1 lb 5 oz) boiling potatoes, peeled and chopped**

**2 tbsp canola or olive oil**

**300 g (10½ oz/2 cups) gluten-free self-raising flour**

**1 tsp gluten-free baking powder**

**1 tsp salt**

**2 eggs**

**Filling**

**40 g (1½ oz) butter**

**1 leek, washed and thinly sliced**

**3 eggs**

**185 ml (6 fl oz/¾ cup) milk**

**185 g (6½ oz/¾ cup) sour cream**

**Prep time** 20 minutes
**Cooking time** 50 minutes
**Makes** 24

**1** Preheat oven to 180°C (350°F/Gas 4). Lightly grease two 12-hole round-based patty pans. Boil or steam potatoes for 15 minutes, or until tender. Drain well, then mash until smooth. You will need 450 g (1 lb/2 cups) warm mashed potato for this recipe.

**2** Combine the mashed potato and oil in a large bowl. Sift in the flour and baking powder, then add the salt and enough egg to mix to a smooth dough. Lightly dust a board with gluten-free flour, then knead the dough on this board until smooth. Roll out pastry until it is 5 mm (¼ in) thick. Cut into 6–7 cm (2½–2¾ in) rounds and place in the prepared pans. Bake for 5 minutes, then remove from the oven and press out any air bubbles in the pastry. Cool completely. Increase the oven temperature to 200°C (400°F/Gas 6).

**3** To make the filling, melt the butter in a heavy-based saucepan over medium heat. Add the leek and cook, stirring often, for 5–6 minutes until tender. Set aside to cool. Season with salt and freshly ground black pepper.

**4** Whisk the eggs, milk and sour cream together in a bowl until well combined. Divide the leek mixture evenly among the pastry cases, then pour the egg mixture over the filling. Bake for 15–20 minutes, or until set and golden brown. Serve hot or cold.

## nutrition per serve (4)   Energy **701 kJ (167 Cal)** Fat **4.7 g** Saturated fat **0.6 g**
Protein **10.2 g** Carbohydrate **17.7 g** Fibre **8.3 g** Cholesterol **0 mg** Sodium **210 g**

# White bean and chickpea dip

**400 g (14 oz) tin cannellini (white) beans** <sup>GF</sup>, **drained and rinsed**

**400 g (14 oz) tin chickpeas** <sup>GF</sup>, **drained and rinsed**

**1½ tsp ground cumin**

**3 garlic cloves, crushed**

**2 tbsp chopped flat-leaf (Italian) parsley**

**3 tbsp lemon juice**

**1 tsp grated lemon zest**

**1 tbsp tahini** <sup>GF</sup>

**1** Place all ingredients in a food processor and process for 30 seconds. With the motor still running, slowly add 3 tablespoons hot water to the processor in a thin stream until the mixture is smooth and 'dippable'. Serve at room temperature with fresh vegetable sticks and gluten-free bread, crackers, rice cakes or toasted pieces of tortilla.

**Prep time** 10 minutes
**Cooking time** Nil
**Serves** 3–4

nutrition per serve (6)   Energy **751 kJ (179 Cal)**  Fat **7.1 g**  Saturated fat **1 g**
Protein **5.2 g**  Carbohydrate **20.9 g**  Fibre **5.8 g**  Cholesterol **0 mg**  Sodium **27 g**

# Roasted buckwheat tabouleh

165 g (5¾ oz/1 cup) roasted
   buckwheat kernels (groats)

300 g (10½ oz/2 large bunches)
   flat-leaf (Italian) parsley

1 handful mint

4 spring onions (scallions), thinly
   sliced

4 tomatoes, finely chopped

2 garlic cloves, crushed

3 tbsp lemon juice

2 tbsp olive oil


**Prep time** 30 minutes +

15 minutes soaking

**Cooking time** Nil

**Serves** 4–6

**1**  Put the buckwheat in a bowl. Pour in enough water to cover the buckwheat and leave to soak for 15 minutes, or until the buckwheat has softened a little. Drain well, then spread onto a clean tea towel (dish towel) to dry.

**2**  Finely chop the parsley and mint with a large knife or in a food processor. If you are using a food processor, take care not to over-process.

**3**  Put the buckwheat, herbs, spring onion and tomato in a large bowl. To make the dressing, combine the garlic, lemon juice and oil in a jar with a tight-fitting lid and shake well. Pour the dressing over the salad and toss well. Refrigerate until required. Return to room temperature to serve.

## nutrition per serve   Energy **1601 kJ (381 Cal)** Fat **12 g** Saturated fat **1.4 g**
Protein **17.4 g** Carbohydrate **51.5 g** Fibre **11.2 g** Cholesterol **4 mg** Sodium **62 g**

# Spicy lentil salad

225 g (8 oz/1 cup heaped) basmati
　　rice

185 g (6½ oz/1 cup) brown lentils

1 tsp ground turmeric

1 tsp ground cinnamon

6 cardamom pods

3 star anise

2 bay leaves

3 tbsp canola or olive oil

1 tbsp lemon juice

250 g (9 oz) broccoli florets

2 carrots, peeled and cut into
　　julienne strips

1 onion, finely chopped

2 garlic cloves, crushed

1 red capsicum (pepper), finely
　　chopped

1 tsp garam masala

1 tsp ground coriander

250 g (9 oz/1⅔ cups) fresh or frozen
　　peas, thawed if frozen

**Dressing**

250 g (9 oz/1 cup) plain yoghurt

1 tbsp lemon juice

1 tbsp chopped mint

1 tsp cumin seeds

**1** Put the rice, lentils, turmeric, cinnamon, cardamom pods, star anise and bay leaves in a saucepan with 750 ml (26 fl oz/3 cups) water. Stir well and bring to the boil. Reduce the heat, cover and simmer gently for 50–60 minutes, or until the liquid is absorbed. Remove the whole spices. Transfer the mixture to a large bowl. Whisk 2 tablespoons of the oil with the lemon juice, then fork through the rice mixture.

**2** Steam or boil the broccoli and carrots until tender. Drain and refresh in cold water.

**3** Heat the remaining oil in a large frying pan and add the onion, garlic and capsicum. Stir-fry for 2–3 minutes, then add the garam masala and coriander and stir-fry for a further 1–2 minutes. Add the cooked vegetables and peas and toss to coat in the spice mixture. Add to the rice and fork through to combine. Cover and refrigerate until cold.

**4** To make the dressing, mix the yoghurt, lemon juice, mint and cumin seeds together, then season with salt and freshly ground black pepper. Spoon the salad into six individual bowls or onto a platter and top with the dressing.

**Prep time** 30 minutes

**Cooking time** 1¼ hours

**Serves** 6

nutrition per serve (6)   Energy **1285 kJ (307 Cal)** Fat **20.4 g** Saturated fat **11.6 g**
Protein **15.7 g** Carbohydrate **15 g** Fibre **0.5 g** Cholesterol **240 mg** Sodium **215 g**

# Rice and cottage cheese pie

100 g (3½ oz/½ cup) white
  long-grain rice

2 tbsp snipped chives

30 g (1 oz) butter, melted

4 tbsp cottage cheese

2 eggs, lightly beaten

**Filling**

60 g (2¼ oz) butter

5 spring onions (scallions), sliced

4 eggs

250 g (9 oz/1 cup) cottage cheese

**Prep time** 40 minutes + cooling
**Cooking time** 1 hour
**Serves** 4–6

**1**  Preheat the oven to 170°C (325°F/Gas 3). Lightly grease a 23 cm (9 in) flan tin or pie plate.

**2**  Bring a large saucepan of water to the boil. Add the rice and cook for 12 minutes, or until very tender, stirring occasionally. Drain and cool. You will need 280 g (10 oz/1½ cups) of cold cooked rice for this recipe. Combine the cooled rice with the chives, butter, cottage cheese and eggs and press into the base and sides of the prepared tin. Chill for 30 minutes.

**3**  Meanwhile, prepare the filling. Melt the butter in a small saucepan over low heat. Add the spring onion and cook for 8–10 minutes, or until soft, but not brown. Remove from the heat. Allow to cool.

**4**  Combine the eggs, cottage cheese and a pinch of salt in a bowl. Add the spring onion mixture and mix well. Pour the filling into the prepared crust. Bake for 40–45 minutes, or until firm and golden brown. Serve hot or cold.

nutrition per serve   Energy **325 kJ (78 Cal)**  Fat **5.3 g**  Saturated fat **1.5 g**
Protein **2.6 g**  Carbohydrate **5 g**  Fibre **0.2 g**  Cholesterol **32 mg**  Sodium **105 g**

# Chicken and leek puffs

**4 tbsp canola or olive oil**

**115 g (4 oz/¾ cup) gluten-free plain (all-purpose) flour**

**¼ tsp bicarbonate of soda (baking soda)**

**¾ tsp gluten-free baking powder**

**3 eggs**

**Chicken and leek filling**

**40 g (1½ oz) butter**

**150 g (5½ oz) boneless, skinless chicken breast**

**½ leek, washed and thinly sliced**

**1 tbsp gluten-free plain (all-purpose) flour**

**3 tbsp milk**

**3 tbsp chicken stock ᴳᶠ (Basics)**

**1 tbsp chopped parsley**

**Prep time** 1 hour
**Cooking time** 40 minutes
**Makes** 24

**1**  Preheat oven to 210°C (415°F/Gas 6–7). Cover two baking trays with baking paper. Pour 250 ml (9 fl oz/ 1 cup) water and the oil into a saucepan and bring to the boil. Remove from the heat, add the sifted dry ingredients, then return to the heat and stir constantly until the mixture thickens and leaves the side of the saucepan (it may look a little oily). Scoop into the small bowl of an electric mixer and set aside to cool slightly.

**2**  Beat the mixture, adding the eggs one at a time and beating well between each addition, until it is thick and shiny. Place level tablespoons of the mixture onto the prepared trays. Spray lightly all over with cold water, to aid rising. Bake for 10 minutes, or until they rise and start to brown. Reduce the heat to 190°C (375°F/Gas 5) and bake for 10–15 minutes, or until cooked through. Remove the puffs from the oven and leave to cool on a wire rack.

**3**  To make chicken and leek filling, melt 1 tablespoon of butter in a frying pan over medium heat, add chicken breast and fry for 3 minutes on each side, or until cooked through. Remove from pan and cut into small pieces. Melt remaining butter in a saucepan, add leek and cook, stirring often, for 5–6 minutes, or until soft. Sprinkle the flour over the leek and cook, stirring, for 20 seconds. Add combined milk and stock, stirring over heat until mixture boils and thickens. Season with a little salt and pepper. Add the chicken and parsley to the sauce and heat gently until warmed through.

**4**  Split the puffs in half, spoon in the warm filling, then replace the tops. Serve while warm.

## nutrition per serve (4)  Energy **728 kJ (174 Cal)**  Fat **9.7 g**  Saturated fat **1.3 g**
Protein **7.1 g**  Carbohydrate **12.4 g**  Fibre **5.9 g**  Cholesterol **0 mg**  Sodium **53 g**

# Cannellini bean and rocket salad

3 red capsicums (peppers), halved and seeded

1 garlic clove, crushed

grated zest of 1 lemon

2 handfuls coarsely chopped flat-leaf (Italian) parsley

400 g (14 oz) tin cannellini (white) beans <sup>GF</sup>, drained and rinsed

2 tbsp lemon juice

2 tbsp extra-virgin olive oil

100 g (3½ oz/1 small bunch) rocket (arugula) or mixed salad leaves

**Prep time** 20 minutes

**Cooking time** 15 minutes

**Serves** 2 as a main course or 4 as a starter

**1**  Preheat a grill (broiler) to medium. Roast the capsicums, skin side up, until the skin blackens and blisters. Set aside in a plastic bag for 5 minutes, then peel away the skin and slice the flesh into strips.

**2**  Combine the garlic, lemon zest and parsley in a bowl.

**3**  Put the cannellini beans in a bowl and add half of the parsley mixture, 1 tablespoon lemon juice, 1 tablespoon extra-virgin olive oil and salt and pepper to taste. Toss together. Place the rocket or salad leaves on a large plate and dress with the remaining lemon juice and extra-virgin olive oil.

**4**  Scatter the bean mixture over the leaves, then lay the capsicum strips on top, along with the remaining parsley mixture. Season with salt and pepper and serve immediately.

nutrition per serve   Energy **638 kJ (151 Cal)** Fat **9.9 g** Saturated fat **1.3 g**
Protein **7.3 g** Carbohydrate **4.8 g** Fibre **6.2 g** Cholesterol **0 mg** Sodium **15 g**

# Roast mushroom and bean salad

**600 g (1 lb 5 oz) field mushrooms, brushed clean**

**2 tbsp olive oil**

**3 garlic cloves, crushed**

**2 tbsp lemon juice**

**6 French shallots, root ends trimmed, skin left on**

**1½ tbsp tarragon vinegar**

**2 tsp finely chopped tarragon**

**1 tbsp finely chopped flat-leaf (Italian) parsley**

**200 g (7 oz) baby green beans, trimmed**

**2 handfuls rocket (arugula)**

**Prep time** 15 minutes
**Cooking time** 35 minutes
**Serves** 4

**1** Preheat the oven to 200°C (400°F/Gas 6). Place the mushrooms in a single layer in a large roasting tin. Add the oil, garlic, lemon juice and shallots and gently toss until coated. Roast for 30 minutes, occasionally spooning over the juices. Remove from the oven and cool to room temperature. Slip the shallots from their skins and discard the skin.

**2** Pour the cooking juices into a large mixing bowl. Add the tarragon vinegar, tarragon and parsley. Mix and season well.

**3** Blanch the beans in boiling salted water for 2 minutes, or until just tender. Drain well and, while still hot, add to the dressing. Set aside to cool to room temperature.

**4** Cut the mushrooms into quarters, or eighths if large, and add to the beans along with the shallots and rocket. Gently toss together and serve on a platter or four individual plates.

nutrition per serve   Energy **837 kJ (200 Cal)**  Fat **6.2 g**  Saturated fat **1.1 g**
Protein **6.2 g**  Carbohydrate **27.7 g**  Fibre **7 g**  Cholesterol **25 mg**  Sodium **1715 g**

# Potato and pumpkin soup

1 tbsp canola or olive oil

1 leek, halved lengthways, washed and sliced

2 garlic cloves, crushed

500 g (1 lb 2 oz) all-purpose potatoes, peeled and chopped

500 g (1 lb 2 oz) butternut pumpkin (squash), peeled, seeded and chopped

1.25 litres (44 fl oz/5 cups) vegetable stock ᴳᶠ (Basics)

snipped chives, to serve

gluten-free bread, to serve

**Prep time** 30 minutes
**Cooking time** 40 minutes
**Serves** 4

**1**  Heat the oil in a large saucepan over medium heat. Add the leek and garlic and cook, stirring, for 2 minutes. Reduce the heat to low. Cover the pan with a lid and cook, stirring occasionally, for 7–8 minutes, or until the leek is very soft.

**2**  Add the potato, pumpkin and stock to the pan. Bring to the boil. Reduce the heat and simmer, partially covered, for 20–25 minutes, or until the vegetables are very soft. Set the pan aside for 10 minutes to allow the mixture to cool slightly.

**3**  Purée the soup in a blender or food processor (in batches, if necessary) until smooth. Divide the soup among four bowls and sprinkle with chives. Serve with gluten-free bread.

nutrition per serve    Energy **1487 kJ (355 Cal)**  Fat **12.7 g**  Saturated fat **2 g**
Protein **36 g**  Carbohydrate **21.8 g**  Fibre **4.8 g**  Cholesterol **81 mg**  Sodium **1509 g**

# Fish and bean soup

**2 tbsp canola or olive oil**

**1 large leek, washed and thinly sliced**

**500 g (1 lb 2 oz) boiling potatoes, peeled and chopped**

**2 garlic cloves, crushed**

**1.5 litres (52 fl oz/6 cups) chicken stock GF (Basics)**

**250 g (9 oz) green beans, cut into 3 cm (1¼ in) pieces**

**500 g (1 lb 2 oz) firm white boneless fish, cut into small cubes**

**3 spring onions (scallions), thinly sliced on the diagonal**

**1** Heat the oil in a large saucepan over medium heat. Cook the leek, stirring often, for 5–6 minutes, or until it softens.

**2** Add the potato and garlic and cook, stirring, for 2 minutes. Pour in the stock, increase the heat to high and bring to the boil. Reduce the heat and simmer, partially covered, for 10 minutes, or until the potato is almost tender when tested with the point of a knife.

**3** Add the beans and fish and continue to cook for a further 5 minutes, or until the fish and beans are cooked. Stir in the spring onions. Season to taste with salt and pepper.

**Prep time** 15 minutes

**Cooking time** 30 minutes

**Serves** 4

**nutrition per serve** Energy 972 kJ (232 Cal) Fat 2.8 g Saturated fat 0.4 g
Protein 17.3 g Carbohydrate 30.5 g Fibre 10 g Cholesterol 5 mg Sodium 1181 g

# Red lentil and parsnip soup

1 tsp olive oil

1 onion, chopped

2 garlic cloves, crushed

1 parsnip, peeled and chopped

1 celery stalk, chopped

1 large carrot, peeled and chopped

1 tsp ground cumin

1 tbsp tomato paste (concentrated purée) GF

400 g (14 oz) tin diced tomatoes

185 g (6½ oz/¾ cup) red lentils

1 litre (35 fl oz/4 cups) chicken or vegetable stock GF
   (Basics) or water

1 tbsp lemon juice

1 handful chopped flat-leaf (Italian) parsley

gluten-free bread, to serve

**1** Heat the oil in a large, heavy-based saucepan. Add the onion and garlic and stir-fry for 2 minutes, or until softened. Add the parsnip, celery and carrot and cook, covered, over low heat for 8 minutes to sweat the vegetables. Stir once or twice, taking care not to brown.

**2** Stir in the cumin, tomato paste, tomatoes, lentils and stock or water. Bring to the boil, then reduce the heat and simmer for 20 minutes, or until the lentils are cooked. Season well with salt and pepper. Stir in the lemon juice and parsley. Serve with gluten-free bread.

**Prep time** 20 minutes
**Cooking time** 30 minutes
**Serves** 4

nutrition per serve   Energy **1367 kJ (326 Cal)** Fat **6.1 g** Saturated fat **2.4 g**
Protein **31.2 g** Carbohydrate **35.9 g** Fibre **2.5 g** Cholesterol **64 mg** Sodium **2968 g**

# Vietnamese beef soup

**400 g (14 oz) lean rump steak, trimmed**

**½ onion**

**1½ tbsp fish sauce** GF

**1 star anise**

**1 cinnamon stick**

**pinch of ground white pepper**

**1.5 litres (52 fl oz/6 cups) beef stock** GF **(Basics)**

**300 g (10½ oz) thin fresh rice noodles**

**3 spring onions (scallions), thinly sliced**

**1 small handful Vietnamese mint**

**90 g (3¼ oz/1 cup) bean sprouts, trimmed**

**1 small onion, halved and thinly sliced**

**1 small red chilli, thinly sliced on the diagonal**

**lemon wedges, to serve**

**1** Wrap the steak in plastic wrap and freeze for 40 minutes. Freezing the meat will make it easier to slice.

**2** Meanwhile, put the onion half, fish sauce, star anise, cinnamon stick, white pepper, stock and 500 ml (17 fl oz/2 cups) water in a large saucepan. Bring to the boil, then reduce the heat, cover and simmer for 20 minutes. Discard the onion, star anise and cinnamon stick.

**3** Put the noodles in a large heatproof bowl. Cover with boiling water and soak for 5 minutes, or until softened. Separate gently and drain. Thinly slice the meat across the grain.

**4** Divide the noodles and spring onion among four deep bowls. Top with the beef, mint, bean sprouts, thinly sliced onion and chilli. Ladle the hot broth over the top and serve with the lemon wedges—the heat of the liquid will cook the beef.

**Prep time** 20 minutes + 40 minutes freezing

**Cooking time** 30 minutes

**Serves** 4

# Main meals

nutrition per serve   Energy **2927 kJ (697 Cal)** Fat **7.4 g** Saturated fat **0.9 g**
Protein **30.4 g** Carbohydrate **129.4 g** Fibre **21.9 g** Cholesterol **0 mg** Sodium **1025 g**

# Three bean chilli with rice

2 tsp canola or olive oil

1 large onion, finely chopped

3 garlic cloves, crushed

2 tbsp ground cumin

1 tbsp ground coriander

1 tsp ground cinnamon

1 tsp chilli powder

400 g (14 oz) tin diced tomatoes

375 ml (13 fl oz/1½ cups) vegetable
   stock <sup>GF</sup> (Basics)

400 g (14 oz) tin chickpeas <sup>GF</sup>,
   drained and rinsed

400 g (14 oz) tin red kidney beans <sup>GF</sup>,
   drained and rinsed

400 g (14 oz) tin cannellini (white)
   beans <sup>GF</sup>, drained and rinsed

2 tbsp tomato paste (concentrated
   purée) <sup>GF</sup>

2 tsp sugar

400 g (14 oz/2 cups) basmati rice,
   rinsed and drained

**1** Heat the oil in a large frying pan and cook the onion over medium–low heat for 5 minutes, or until golden, stirring frequently. Reduce the heat, add the garlic, cumin, coriander, cinnamon and chilli powder, then stir for 1 minute.

**2** Add the tomatoes, stock, chickpeas, kidney beans and cannellini beans and combine with the onion mixture. Bring to the boil, then simmer for 20 minutes, stirring occasionally. Add the tomato paste and sugar and season to taste with salt and freshly ground black pepper. Simmer for a further 5 minutes.

**3** Meanwhile, put the rice and 1 litre (35 fl oz/4 cups) water in a saucepan and bring to the boil over medium heat. Reduce the heat to low, cover with a lid and cook for 20 minutes, or until the rice is tender. Remove from the heat and leave to stand, covered, for 5 minutes. Serve with the bean chilli. As a treat, grate some cheese over the top when serving.

**Prep time** 20 minutes

**Cooking time** 35 minutes

**Serves** 4

**nutrition per serve**  Energy **1933 kJ (460 Cal)**  Fat **13.1 g**  Saturated fat **5.3 g**
Protein **51 g**  Carbohydrate **23 g**  Fibre **10.7 g**  Cholesterol **113 mg**  Sodium **589 g**

# Lamb casserole with beans

**300 g (10½ oz/1½ cups) dried borlotti or red kidney beans**

**1 kg (2 lb 4 oz) lean boned leg of lamb**

**2 tsp olive oil**

**50 g (1¾ oz) low-fat bacon slices <sup>GF</sup>, chopped**

**1 large onion, chopped**

**2 garlic cloves, crushed**

**1 large carrot, peeled and chopped**

**500 ml (17 fl oz/2 cups) red wine**

**1 tbsp tomato paste (concentrated purée) <sup>GF</sup>**

**375 ml (13 fl oz/1½ cups) beef stock<sup>GF</sup> (Basics)**

**2 large sprigs of rosemary**

**2 sprigs of thyme**

**Prep time** 25 minutes + overnight soaking

**Cooking time** 2¼ hours

**Serves** 6

**1**  Put the beans in a large bowl, cover with water and leave to soak overnight. Drain well.

**2**  Preheat the oven to 160°C (315°F/Gas 2–3). Trim any fat from the lamb and cut into bite-sized cubes.

**3**  Heat the oil in a large flameproof casserole dish over high heat and brown the lamb in two batches for 2 minutes. Remove all the lamb from the dish and set aside. Add the bacon and onion to the casserole dish. Cook over medium heat for 3 minutes, or until the onion is soft. Add the garlic and carrot and cook for 1 minute, or until fragrant.

**4**  Return the lamb and any juices to the pan, increase the heat to high and add the wine. Bring to the boil and cook for 2 minutes. Add the beans, tomato paste, stock, rosemary and thyme, bring to the boil, then cover and cook in the oven for 2 hours, or until the meat is tender. Stir occasionally during cooking and skim off any fat from the surface. Season with salt and freshly ground black pepper and remove the herb sprigs before serving.

**nutrition per serve** Energy **2871 kJ (683 Cal)** Fat **13.8 g** Saturated fat **3.6 g**
Protein **40.3 g** Carbohydrate **98 g** Fibre **7.5 g** Cholesterol **116 mg** Sodium **431 g**

# Chilli con pollo

2 tsp olive oil

1 onion, finely chopped

500 g (1 lb 2 oz) lean minced (ground) chicken

1–2 tsp mild chilli powder

400 g (14 oz) tin diced tomatoes

2 tbsp tomato paste (concentrated purée) <sup>GF</sup>

400 g (14 oz) tin red kidney beans <sup>GF</sup>, drained and rinsed

400 g (14 oz/2 cups) basmati rice, drained and rinsed

4 tbsp chopped parsley

250 g (9 oz/1 cup) low-fat plain yoghurt

**Prep time** 10 minutes
**Cooking time** 1 hour
**Serves** 4

**1** Heat oil in a large saucepan. Add onion and cook over medium heat for 3 minutes, or until soft. Increase heat and add chicken. Cook until browned, breaking up any lumps with a wooden spoon.

**2** Add chilli powder and cook for 1 minute. Add tomato, tomato paste and 125 ml (4 fl oz/½ cup) water and stir well. Bring to boil, then reduce the heat and simmer for 30 minutes. Stir in kidney beans and heat through. Season to taste with salt and black pepper.

**3** Meanwhile, put the rice and 1 litre (35 fl oz/4 cups) water in a saucepan and bring to the boil over medium heat. Reduce the heat to low, cover with a lid and cook for 20 minutes, or until the rice is tender. Remove from the heat and leave to stand, covered, for 5 minutes.

**4** Sprinkle the chilli con pollo with the parsley and serve with the yoghurt and rice.

nutrition per serve  Energy **2485 kJ (592 Cal)** Fat **6.5 g** Saturated fat **1.6 g** Protein **41.1 g** Carbohydrate **91.8 g** Fibre **5.1 g** Cholesterol **119 mg** Sodium **664 g**

# Hungarian pork and lentil stew

2 tsp olive oil

2 onions, chopped

500 g (1 lb 2 oz) lean diced pork

2 tsp sweet paprika

1 tsp hot paprika

½ tsp dried thyme

2 tbsp tomato paste (concentrated purée) GF

1 tsp soft brown sugar

3 tbsp red lentils

375 ml (13 fl oz/1½ cups) beef stock GF (Basics)

1 tomato

400 g (14 oz/2 cups) basmati rice, rinsed and drained

2 tbsp low-fat plain yoghurt

**Prep time** 20 minutes

**Cooking time** 1 hour 5 minutes

**Serves** 4

1  Heat the olive oil in a large, deep saucepan over high heat. Add the onion, pork and paprika and stir for 3–4 minutes, or until browned.

2  Add the thyme, tomato paste, sugar, lentils and stock and season with salt and freshly ground black pepper. Bring to the boil, reduce the heat to very low and cook, covered, for 20 minutes, stirring occasionally to prevent sticking. Uncover and cook for 15–20 minutes, or until thickened.

3  Remove from the heat and set aside for 10 minutes. To prepare the tomato, cut it in half and scoop out the seeds. Slice the flesh into thin strips.

4  Meanwhile, put the rice and 1 litre (35 fl oz/4 cups) water in a saucepan and bring to the boil over medium heat. Reduce the heat to low, cover with a lid and cook for 20 minutes, or until the rice is tender. Remove from the heat and leave to stand, covered, for 5 minutes.

5  Just before serving, stir the yoghurt into the stew. Scatter with tomato. Serve with the rice and a salad.

**nutrition per serve**   Energy **1531 kJ (366 Cal)** Fat **5.2 g** Saturated **fat 0.9 g**
Protein **17.6 g** Carbohydrate **57.1 g** Fibre **11.6 g** Cholesterol **0 mg** Sodium **900 g**

# Vegetarian paella

200 g (7 oz/1 cup) dried haricot
beans

¼ tsp saffron threads

2 tsp olive oil

1 onion, diced

1 red capsicum (pepper), cut into
thin strips

5 garlic cloves, crushed

275 g (9¾ oz/1¼ cups) paella or
arborio rice

1 tbsp sweet paprika

½ tsp mixed spice

750 ml (26 fl oz/3 cups) vegetable
stock GF (Basics)

400 g (14 oz) tin diced tomatoes

1½ tbsp tomato paste (concentrated
purée) GF

140 g (5 oz/2⅓ cups) fresh or frozen
soya beans

100 g (3½ oz) silverbeet (Swiss
chard), shredded

400 g (14 oz) tin artichoke hearts in
brine, drained and rinsed

4 tbsp chopped coriander (cilantro)
leaves

**1**  Put the haricot beans in a large bowl, cover with cold
water and leave to soak overnight. Drain and rinse well.

**2**  Place the saffron threads in a small frying pan over
medium–low heat. Dry-fry, shaking for 1 minute, or
until darkened. Remove from the heat and, when cool,
crumble into a small bowl. Pour in 125 ml (4 fl oz/
½ cup) warm water and allow to steep.

**3**  Heat the oil in a large paella pan or frying pan. Add the
onion and capsicum and cook over medium–high heat
for 5 minutes, or until the onion softens. Stir in the
garlic and cook for 1 minute. Reduce the heat and add
the drained beans, rice, paprika, mixed spice and
season with salt. Stir to coat. Add the saffron water,
stock, tomatoes and tomato paste and bring to the boil.
Cover, reduce the heat and simmer for 20 minutes.

**4**  Stir in the soya beans, silverbeet and artichoke hearts
and cook, covered, for 8 minutes, or until all the liquid
is absorbed and the rice and beans are tender. Turn off
the heat and leave for 5 minutes. Stir in the coriander
just before serving.

**Prep time** 20 minutes + overnight soaking
**Cooking time** 40 minutes
**Serves** 6

nutrition per serve   Energy **2291 kJ (545 Cal)** Fat **5.8 g** Saturated fat **0.8 g**
Protein **33.2 g** Carbohydrate **88.7 g** Fibre **4.7 g** Cholesterol **118 mg** Sodium **1022 g**

# Warm prawn and scallop stir-fry

400 g (14 oz/2 cups) basmati rice,
  rinsed and drained

2 tsp five-spice

1–2 small red chillies, seeded and
  finely chopped

2–3 garlic cloves, crushed

2 tsp sesame oil

500 g (1 lb 2 oz) raw prawns
  (shrimp), peeled and deveined,
  tails intact

300 g (10½ oz) scallops, trimmed,
  with coral intact

200 g (7 oz) asparagus, trimmed and
  cut into short lengths

150 g (5½ oz) snow peas
  (mangetout), trimmed

125 g (4½ oz/2¾ cups) roughly
  chopped rocket (arugula)

2 tbsp tamari GF

2 tbsp lemon juice

1 tbsp mirin

2 tsp honey

6 spring onions (scallions), sliced

1 tbsp chopped coriander (cilantro)
  leaves

1 tbsp sesame seeds, toasted

**1**  Put the rice and 1 litre (35 fl oz/4 cups) water in a
saucepan and bring to the boil over medium heat.
Reduce the heat to low, cover with a lid and cook for
20 minutes, or until the rice is tender. Remove from the
heat and leave to stand, covered, for 5 minutes.

**2**  Meanwhile, combine the five-spice, chilli, garlic and
sesame oil in a large non-metallic bowl. Add the prawns
and scallops and toss to coat. Cover with plastic wrap
and refrigerate for at least 10 minutes.

**3**  Blanch the asparagus and snow peas. Drain and plunge
into a bowl of iced water, then drain again. Arrange on
four plates with the rocket. Combine the tamari, lemon
juice, mirin and honey in a small bowl.

**4**  Heat a wok over high heat, add the seafood and spring
onions in batches and cook for 3–4 minutes, or until
cooked through, reheating the wok between batches.
Remove from the wok and set aside. Add the tamari–
lemon sauce and coriander to the wok, then bring to
the boil. Cook over high heat for 1–2 minutes. Return
the seafood to the wok and toss well. Divide among the
plates and sprinkle with the sesame seeds. Serve with
the rice.

**Prep time** 30 minutes + 10 minutes marinating
**Cooking time** 35 minutes
**Serves** 4

# Chicken, sprouts and noodles

300 g (10½ oz) dried mung bean
    vermicelli

500 g (1 lb 2 oz) boneless, skinless
    chicken breast

2 tsp canola or olive oil

1 onion, thinly sliced

3 makrut (kaffir lime) leaves,
    shredded

1 red capsicum (pepper), sliced

70 g (2½ oz) snow peas (mangetout),
    trimmed

3 tbsp lime juice

100 ml (3½ fl oz) tamari GF

50 g (1¾ oz) snow pea (mangetout)
    sprouts, trimmed

2 tbsp chopped coriander (cilantro)
    leaves

**Prep time** 15 minutes +
10 minutes soaking
**Cooking time** 30 minutes
**Serves** 4

**1** Put the noodles in a large bowl and cover with warm water. Soak for 10 minutes, or until they are translucent. Drain. Transfer to a saucepan of boiling water and cook for 10 minutes, or until tender. Rinse under cold water and drain.

**2** Meanwhile, trim the chicken and cut into thin slices. Heat a wok over medium heat, add the oil and swirl to coat. Add the onion and kaffir lime leaves and stir-fry for 3–5 minutes, or until the onion begins to soften. Remove from the wok. Add the chicken in batches and cook for a further 4 minutes, or until lightly browned. Remove from the wok and set aside. Reheat the wok between batches.

**3** Return the onion mixture and all the chicken to the wok, add the capsicum and snow peas and continue to cook for 2–3 minutes. Stir in the lime juice, tamari and 2 tablespoons water and cook for 1–2 minutes, or until sauce reduces slightly. Add noodles and toss through mixture to warm through. Add sprouts and coriander and cook until the sprouts have wilted slightly.

nutrition per serve   Energy **2717 kJ (649 Cal)**  Fat **31.8 g**  Saturated fat **19.2 g**
Protein **42.2 g**  Carbohydrate **48.4 g**  Fibre **1.8 g**  Cholesterol **249 mg**  Sodium **1769 g**

# Chicken and leek pie

**350 g (12 oz) boneless, skinless chicken breast**

**30 g (1 oz) butter**

**1 leek, washed and thinly sliced**

**1 celery stalk, thinly sliced**

**4 slices of low-fat bacon GF, thinly sliced**

**2 tsp pure maize cornflour (cornstarch) GF**

**185 ml (6 fl oz/¾ cup) low-fat milk**

**1 egg yolk**

**1 small handful parsley, chopped**

**125 g (4½ oz/1 cup firmly packed) grated low-fat cheddar cheese GF**

**1 quantity gluten-free shortcrust pastry (Basics)**

**Prep time** 30 minutes +
20 minutes standing
**Cooking time** 55 minutes
**Serves** 4

**1**  To make filling, put chicken in a saucepan and cover with cold water. Slowly bring to boil, then simmer for 2 minutes. Turn off heat, cover and set aside 20 minutes.

**2**  Heat butter in a medium frying pan. Add leek, celery and bacon. Cook, stirring occasionally for 5 minutes over low heat until leek is soft. In a small bowl combine cornflour with a little of the milk. Mix until smooth. Add the remaining milk and egg yolk. Pour over the leek mixture. Stir over a low heat for 2–3 minutes until thickened. Season with salt and pepper.

**3**  Shred the chicken with a fork, then stir it into the leek mixture. Transfer to a plate to cool completely, then stir in the parsley. Preheat the oven to 200°C (400°F/Gas 6).

**4**  Lightly grease a 23 cm (9 in) fluted flan tin, then line it with the prepared pastry. Trim to fit the tin. The pastry is soft and malleable so just fill any tears and cracks if necessary. Reserve the leftover dough.

**5**  Place the tin on a baking tray. Cover the pastry with a sheet of baking paper and half fill with baking beads or rice. Bake for 10 minutes. Remove the beads and paper and bake for a further 10–15 minutes, or until lightly browned. Fill any cracks with small amounts of reserved pastry. Bake for a further 2 minutes to set. Remove from the oven and cool completely. Reduce the oven temperature to 180°C (350°F/Gas 4).

**6**  Fill the cooled pastry with the cooled filling. Scatter the cheese over the top. Bake for 20 minutes until cooked and the pastry is golden brown.

# Beans and capsicum stir-fry

2 tsp canola or olive oil

2 garlic cloves, crushed

1 red onion, cut into thin wedges

1 red capsicum (pepper), cut into
short, thin strips

1 yellow capsicum (pepper), cut into
short, thin strips

400 g (14 oz) tin chickpeas [GF],
drained and rinsed

400 g (14 oz) tin red kidney beans [GF],
drained and rinsed

1 tsp soft brown sugar

2 tbsp balsamic vinegar

3 tbsp lime juice

250 g (9 oz) cherry tomatoes, halved

1 Lebanese (short) cucumber,
chopped

3 tbsp chopped coriander (cilantro)
leaves

butter lettuce leaves, to serve

**1**  Heat a wok until very hot, add the oil and swirl to coat.
Add the garlic, onion and red and yellow capsicum
strips and stir-fry over medium heat for 2–3 minutes.
Remove from the wok and set aside.

**2**  Add the chickpeas and kidney beans to the wok, stir
in the brown sugar and balsamic vinegar and toss for
2–3 minutes, or until the liquid has reduced by half.
Add the lime juice and toss until well combined.

**3**  Using two wooden spoons, stir in the cherry tomatoes,
cucumber, coriander and the onion and capsicum
mixture. Stir-fry briefly until heated through and
thoroughly mixed. Put a couple of lettuce leaves on each
plate and spoon the stir-fry onto the leaves to serve.

**Prep time** 15 minutes

**Cooking time:** 10 minutes

**Serves** 6

**nutrition per serve** Energy **2743 kJ (653 Cal)** Fat **8.2 g** Saturated fat **4.1 g**
Protein **53.9 g** Carbohydrate **89 g** Fibre **2.7 g** Cholesterol **142 mg** Sodium **407 g**

# Tandoori fish cutlets

4 firm white fish cutlets

3 tbsp lemon juice

1 onion, finely chopped

2 garlic cloves, crushed

1 tbsp grated fresh ginger

1 red chilli

1 tbsp garam masala

1 tsp paprika

¼ tsp salt

500 g (1 lb 2 oz/2 cups) low-fat plain yoghurt

400 g (14 oz/2 cups) basmati rice, rinsed and drained

**1** Pat fish cutlets dry with paper towels and arrange in a shallow non-metallic dish. Drizzle lemon juice over fish.

**2** To make marinade, blend onion, garlic, ginger, chilli, garam masala, paprika and salt until smooth. Transfer to a bowl and stir in yoghurt. Spoon over fish and turn to coat thoroughly. Cover and refrigerate overnight.

**3** Put rice and 1 litre (35 fl oz/4 cups) water in a saucepan and bring to boil. Reduce heat to low, cover with a lid and cook for 20 minutes. Remove from heat and leave to stand, covered, for 5 minutes.

**4** Meanwhile, heat a grill (broiler). Remove cutlets from marinade and allow any excess to drip off. Cook cutlets under the grill or on the barbecue for 3–4 minutes on each side, or until the fish flakes easily when tested with a fork. Serve with the rice.

**Prep time** 20 minutes +
overnight marinating
**Cooking time** 30 minutes
**Serves** 4

nutrition per serve  Energy **2006 kJ (479 Cal)** Fat **8.4 g**  Saturated fat **2.7 g**
Protein **45.5 g** Carbohydrate **46.7 g** Fibre **16.5 g** Cholesterol **102 g** Sodium **746 g**

# Herbed lamb with vegetables

6 large carrots, peeled and cut into
    2 cm (¾ in) pieces on the diagonal

canola or olive oil spray

2 tbsp Dijon mustard GF

2 tbsp finely chopped flat-leaf
    (Italian) parsley

1 tsp finely chopped thyme

1 tsp finely chopped sage

3 garlic cloves, crushed

2 x 300 g (10½ oz) pieces lamb rump
    or mini lamb roasts, trimmed

750 g (1 lb 10 oz) small new potatoes

250 ml (9 fl oz/1 cup) vegetable
    stock GF (Basics)

625 g (1 lb 6 oz/4 cups) frozen peas,
    thawed

2 tbsp mint

**Prep time** 20 minutes
**Cooking time** 1 hour
**Serves** 4

1  Preheat the oven to 200°C (400°F/Gas 6). Spray the carrots with the oil, season well and place into a large roasting tin (you will be adding the lamb pieces halfway through cooking). Cook in the oven for 1 hour, or until golden and soft.

2  Place the mustard, parsley, thyme, sage and 2 of the crushed garlic cloves in a bowl. Mix well to combine and add the lamb pieces. Thoroughly coat with the mixture and add to the carrots in the roasting tin 30 minutes before it is due to be ready.

3  Meanwhile, cook the new potatoes in a large saucepan of boiling water for 12 minutes, or until tender. Drain.

4  In a small saucepan over high heat, bring the vegetable stock to the boil with the remaining crushed garlic clove. Add the peas and cook for 3 minutes. Remove from the heat and strain, reserving the stock. Put the peas, mint and reserved stock in a food processor. Blend until smooth, then season to taste.

5  Remove lamb from the oven and allow to rest, covered, on a board for 5 minutes before slicing across the grain. Divide among four plates and serve with boiled potatoes, pea and mint purée and roasted carrots.

# Tuna kebabs with chickpea salsa

**Salsa**

**2 tsp olive oil**

**2–3 small red chillies, seeded and finely chopped**

**3–4 garlic cloves, crushed**

**1 red onion, finely chopped**

**3 tomatoes, seeded and chopped**

**3 tbsp dry white wine or water**

**2 x 300 g (10½ oz) tins chickpeas GF, drained and rinsed**

**3 tbsp chopped oregano**

**4 tbsp chopped parsley**

**1 kg (2 lb 4 oz) tuna fillet**

**canola or olive oil spray**

**lemon wedges, to serve**

**Prep time** 20 minutes

**Cooking time** 20 minutes

**Serves** 4

1  To make the salsa, heat the oil in a large saucepan, add the chilli, garlic and onion and stir for 5 minutes, or until softened. Add the tomato and wine or water. Cook over low heat for 10 minutes, or until the mixture is soft, pulpy and the liquid has evaporated. Stir in the chickpeas, oregano and parsley. Season with salt and freshly ground black pepper.

2  Meanwhile, trim the tuna and cut into 4 cm (1½ in) cubes. Heat a chargrill pan or barbecue hotplate. Thread the tuna onto eight metal skewers, lightly spray with the oil, then cook, turning, for 3 minutes. Do not overcook or the tuna will fall apart. Serve with the salsa and lemon wedges.

**nutrition per serve**   Energy **2687 kJ (642 Cal)**  Fat **27.1 g**  Saturated fat **6.5 g**
Protein **66.9 g**  Carbohydrate **27.9 g**  Fibre **8.1 g**  Cholesterol **313 mg**  Sodium **574 g**

# Crunchy coated chicken

80 g (2¾ oz/½ cup) gluten-free plain
   (all-purpose) flour

2 eggs

90 g (3¼ oz/1 cup) rice bran

2–3 tbsp poppy seeds

10 (2 kg/4 lb 8 oz) chicken pieces,
   skin removed

canola or olive oil spray


**Prep time** 20 minutes +
30 minutes refrigeration
**Cooking time** 30 minutes
**Serves** 4

**1**  Preheat the oven to 200°C (400°F/Gas 6). Lightly grease
a baking tray.

**2**  Put the flour in a shallow bowl. Mix the eggs with
2 tablespoons water in a separate bowl and mix the
bran, poppy seeds and a little salt in a third bowl. Dust
the chicken pieces lightly with the flour. Dip them in
the combined egg and water, then roll in the bran
mixture, pressing the mixture on firmly. Put the chicken
pieces on the prepared tray and refrigerate for
30 minutes to firm the coating.

**3**  Spray the chicken all over with oil spray. Bake for about
30 minutes, or until golden brown and cooked through
when tested.

**4**  Meanwhile, to make the chive yoghurt, combine the
yoghurt and chives in a small bowl, then season to taste
with salt.

**5**  Serve the chicken hot or cold with the chive yoghurt.

# Spicy stew with dal

**Dal**

140 g (5 oz/²⁄₃ cup) yellow split peas

5 cm (2 in) piece of fresh ginger, grated

2–3 garlic cloves, crushed

1 red chilli, seeded and chopped

3 tomatoes

1 red onion

¼ cauliflower

3 slender eggplants (aubergines)

2 carrots, peeled

## nutrition per serve
Energy **858 kJ (204 Cal)** Fat **4.3 g** Saturated fat **0.5 g** Protein **14.1 g** Carbohydrate **27.8 g** Fibre **10 g** Cholesterol **0 mg** Sodium **545 g**

2 small zucchini (courgettes)

2 tsp canola or olive oil

1 tsp yellow mustard seeds

1 tsp cumin seeds

1 tsp ground cumin

½ tsp garam masala

375 ml (13 fl oz/1½ cups) vegetable stock GF (Basics)

80 g (2¾ oz/½ cup) frozen peas, thawed

1 large handful coriander (cilantro) leaves

**Prep time** 25 minutes + 2 hours soaking

**Cooking time 1½ hours**

**Serves 4**

**1** To make the dal, put the split peas in a bowl, cover with water and soak for 2 hours. Drain. Put in a large saucepan with the ginger, garlic, chilli and 750 ml (26 fl oz/3 cups) water. Bring to the boil, then reduce the heat and simmer for 40 minutes, or until just soft.

**2** Meanwhile, prepare the vegetables. To peel the tomatoes, score a cross in the base of each one. Cover with boiling water for 30 seconds, then plunge into cold water. Drain and peel away the skin from the cross. Scoop out the seeds with a teaspoon and roughly chop the flesh. Cut the onion into thin wedges, cut the cauliflower into florets and thickly slice the eggplants, carrots and zucchini.

**3** Heat the oil in a large saucepan over medium heat. Add the mustard seeds, cumin seeds, ground cumin and garam masala and cook for 30 seconds, or until fragrant. Add the onion and cook for a further 2 minutes, or until the onion is soft. Stir in the tomato, eggplant, carrot and cauliflower.

**4** Add the dal and stock, mix together well and simmer, covered, for 45 minutes, or until the vegetables are tender. Stir occasionally. Add the zucchini and peas during the last 10 minutes of cooking. Stir in the coriander leaves and serve hot.

nutrition per serve (6)   Energy **1867 kJ (446 Cal)**  Fat **5.1 g**  Saturated fat **0.9 g**
Protein **20.6 g**  Carbohydrate **75.8 g**  Fibre **6.2 g**  Cholesterol **110 mg**  Sodium **354 g**

# Seafood pasta

1 tbsp olive oil

1 large onion, cut into thin wedges

2 garlic cloves, crushed

80 g (2¾ oz) button mushrooms,
   thinly sliced

3 ripe tomatoes, roughly chopped

2 x 400 g (14 oz) tins diced tomatoes

1 tbsp tomato paste (concentrated
   purée)<sup>GF</sup>

1 tsp sugar

1 tsp freshly ground black pepper

3 tbsp capers, rinsed, drained and
   chopped

8 medium raw prawns (shrimp),
   peeled and deveined

8 scallops, trimmed

2 small cleaned squid tubes,
   cut into rings

1 large handful flat-leaf (Italian)
   parsley, finely chopped

1 handful basil, shredded

500 g (1 lb 2 oz) gluten-free
   fettuccine or other pasta

freshly grated parmesan cheese,
   to serve (optional)

**1**  Heat the olive oil in a large, deep, heavy-based
saucepan. Add the onion and garlic and cook for
2 minutes, or until softened. Add the mushrooms, fresh
and tinned tomatoes, tomato paste, sugar, pepper,
capers and 250 ml (9 fl oz/1 cup) water. Bring to the
boil, then reduce the heat and simmer for 20 minutes.
Stir in the prawns, scallops and squid, then cook for a
further 2–3 minutes until the seafood is just cooked.
Just before serving, stir in the parsley and basil.

**2**  Meanwhile, cook the pasta in a large saucepan of
boiling salted water for 10 minutes, or according to the
packet instructions, until just tender. Drain well and
return to the saucepan. Toss through the sauce. Divide
into bowls and serve with the grated parmesan cheese,
if you like.

**Prep time** 15 minutes
**Cooking time** 30 minutes
**Serves** 4–6

**nutrition per serve**   Energy **2236 kJ (534 Cal)**  Fat **3.2 g**  Saturated fat **1.1 g**
Protein **39.7 g**  Carbohydrate **84.1 g**  Fibre **1.6 g**  Cholesterol **96 mg**  Sodium **312 g**

# Ginger fish with coriander rice

400 g (14 oz/2 cups) basmati rice, rinsed and drained

4 firm white fish cutlets

5 cm (2 in) piece of fresh ginger, shredded

2 garlic cloves, chopped

2 tsp chopped red chilli

2 tbsp chopped coriander (cilantro) stems and leaves

3 spring onions (scallions), thinly sliced

coriander (cilantro) leaves, chopped, extra

3 tbsp lime juice

1 tbsp fish sauce <sup>GF</sup>

2 tsp honey

**1**  Put rice and 1 litre (35 fl oz/4 cups) water in a saucepan and bring to boil over medium heat. Reduce heat to low, cover with lid and cook for 20 minutes, or until rice is tender. Remove from heat and leave to stand, covered, for 5 minutes.

**2**  Meanwhile, cook fish. Line a large bamboo steamer basket with baking paper. Arrange fish in basket and top with ginger, garlic, chilli and coriander stems and leaves. Cover with lid and steam over a large saucepan of boiling water for 8–10 minutes, without letting the basket touch water. Sprinkle spring onion over fish. Cover and steam for a further 30 seconds.

**3**  Stir extra coriander leaves into rice. Divide rice onto serving plates. Top with fish and pour over combined lime juice, fish sauce and honey.

**Prep time** 20 minutes
**Cooking time** 30 minutes
**Serves** 4

# Spaghetti bolognese

1 tbsp canola or olive oil

1 onion, chopped

2 large garlic cloves, crushed

1 celery stalk, diced

1 carrot, peeled and diced

90 g (3¼ oz) button mushrooms,
   finely chopped

500 g (1 lb 2 oz) lean minced
   (ground) beef

1 tsp dried oregano

250 ml (9 fl oz/1 cup) red wine

250 ml (9 fl oz/1 cup) beef stock <sup>GF</sup>
   (Basics)

2 x 400 g (14 oz) tins diced tomatoes

2 tbsp tomato paste (concentrated
   purée) <sup>GF</sup>

375 g (13 oz) gluten-free spaghetti

freshly grated parmesan cheese, to
   serve

2 tbsp chopped basil

**1**  Heat the oil in a large, non-stick saucepan. Add the onion and cook, stirring occasionally, for 3 minutes. Add the garlic, celery, carrot and mushroom and cook for a further 2 minutes. Add the minced beef and cook over high heat for 5 minutes, or until cooked, breaking up any lumps with the back of a spoon. Add the oregano and wine and cook for 3–4 minutes, or until most of the liquid has evaporated.

**2**  Add the stock, tomatoes and tomato paste and season with salt and pepper. Reduce the heat to low and simmer, covered, for 1 hour, stirring occasionally to prevent it from catching on the bottom. If the sauce is too thin, remove the lid and simmer until reduced and thickened. Cool slightly.

**3**  Meanwhile, cook the spaghetti in a large saucepan of boiling salted water for 10 minutes, or according to the packet instructions, until tender. Drain well. Toss the spaghetti with the sauce and serve with the parmesan and basil.

**Prep time** 20 minutes
**Cooking time** 1½ hours
Serves 4

# Steaks with roast capsicum salad

**750 g (1 lb 10 oz) small new potatoes**

**1 red capsicum (pepper), seeded and quartered**

**100 g (3½ oz) green beans, trimmed and halved**

**500 g (1 lb 2 oz) lean sirloin steak, cut into 4 fillets or 4 x 125 g (4½ oz) fillet steaks**

**250 ml (9 fl oz/1 cup) red wine**

**2 tbsp balsamic vinegar**

**1 tbsp soft brown sugar**

**10 small thyme leaves**

**4 handfuls mixed salad leaves**

**90 g (3¼ oz/½ cup) green olives in brine, pitted and lightly squashed**

**1 tbsp baby capers, rinsed and drained (optional)**

**Prep time** 20 minutes
**Cooking time** 25 minutes
**Serves** 4

**1** Put the potatoes in a saucepan of boiling water. Cook for 12 minutes, or until tender, then drain, refresh and cut in half. Set aside.

**2** Meanwhile, preheat a grill (broiler) to medium. Roast the capsicum, skin side up, until the skin blackens and blisters. Set aside in a plastic bag for 5 minutes, then peel away the skin and slice the flesh into thin strips. Blanch the beans for 2 minutes in a saucepan of boiling water. Drain and refresh.

**3** Pat the meat dry with paper towels. Lightly brush a non-stick frying pan with oil and heat to very hot. Add the meat and cook for 2–3 minutes on each side, or until cooked to your liking. Remove from the pan, cover with foil and set aside while preparing the sauce.

**4** Add the wine, vinegar, sugar and half of the thyme leaves to the frying pan. Bring to the boil, stirring continuously. Boil until reduced by about one-third. Set aside until just warm.

**5** Toss together the salad leaves, capsicum and beans in a large bowl. Divide the salad leaves equally onto four large plates. Scatter over the potatoes, olives and capers, if using. Cut the fillets into 1 cm (½ in) thick slices and arrange on top of the salad. Drizzle over the dressing and garnish with the remaining thyme leaves.

nutrition per serve   Energy **1701 kJ (406 Cal)**  Fat **10 g**  Saturated fat **2.8 g**
Protein **32.6 g**  Carbohydrate **44.3 g**  Fibre **2.2 g**  Cholesterol **80 mg**  Sodium **615 g**

# Coriander beef with noodles

4 garlic cloves, finely chopped

1 tbsp finely chopped fresh ginger

1 large handful coriander (cilantro)
    roots, stems and leaves, chopped

3 tsp canola or olive oil

500 g (1 lb 2 oz) lean beef rump steak

400 g (14 oz) fresh rice noodles

1 red onion, thinly sliced

½ red capsicum (pepper), thinly
    sliced

½ green capsicum (pepper), thinly
    sliced

2 tbsp lime juice

2 tbsp tamari GF

1 large handful coriander (cilantro)
    leaves, extra

**Prep time** 20 minutes +

2 hours marinating

**Cooking time** 20 minutes

**Serves** 4

1  To make the marinade, combine garlic, ginger, coriander and 2 teaspoons of oil in a large non-metallic bowl. Trim the beef, then cut into thin strips across the grain. Add to marinade and toss to coat. Cover with plastic wrap and refrigerate for 2 hours or overnight.

2  Put the rice noodles in a large heatproof bowl, cover with boiling water and soak for 8 minutes, or until softened. Separate gently and drain.

3  Heat a wok until very hot and spray with canola or olive oil. Add the meat in three batches and stir-fry for 2–3 minutes, or until the meat is just cooked. Remove all the meat from the wok and keep it warm. Reheat and respray the wok between batches.

4  Heat the remaining 1 teaspoon oil in the wok, add the onion and cook over medium heat for 3–4 minutes, or until slightly softened. Add the capsicum slices and cook, tossing constantly, for a further 3–4 minutes, or until slightly softened.

5  Return all the meat to the wok along with the lime juice, tamari, 2 tablespoons water and extra coriander. Add the noodles. Toss well, then remove from heat and season well with salt and freshly ground black pepper.

# Rogan josh

1 kg (2 lb 4 oz) lean boned leg of lamb

2 tsp canola or olive oil

2 onions, chopped

125 g (4½ oz/½ cup) low-fat plain yoghurt

1 tsp chilli powder

1 tbsp ground coriander

2 tsp ground cumin

1 tsp ground cardamom

1 tsp ground turmeric

½ tsp ground cloves

3 garlic cloves, crushed

1 tbsp grated fresh ginger

400 g (14 oz) tin diced tomatoes

1 tsp salt

3 tbsp slivered almonds

400 g (14 oz/2 cups) basmati rice,
    rinsed and drained

1 tsp garam masala

chopped coriander (cilantro) leaves,
    to serve

**Prep time** 25 minutes

**Cooking time** 2 hours

**Serves** 6

**1**   Trim the lamb of any fat or sinew and cut into small cubes. Heat the oil in a large heavy-based saucepan, add the onion and cook, stirring, for 5 minutes, or until soft. Stir in the yoghurt, chilli powder, coriander, cumin, cardamom, turmeric, cloves, garlic and ginger. Add the tomato and salt and simmer for 5 minutes.

**2**   Add the lamb and stir until coated. Cover and cook over low heat, stirring occasionally, for 1–1½ hours, or until the lamb is tender. Uncover and simmer until the liquid thickens.

**3**   Meanwhile, toast the almonds in a dry frying pan over medium heat for 3–4 minutes, shaking the pan gently, until the nuts are golden brown. Remove from the pan at once to prevent them burning. Put the rice and 1 litre (35 fl oz/4 cups) water in a saucepan and bring to the boil over medium heat. Reduce the heat to low, cover with a lid and cook for 20 minutes, or until the rice is tender. Remove from the heat and leave to stand, covered, for 5 minutes.

**4**   Add the garam masala to the curry and mix through well. Sprinkle the slivered almonds and coriander leaves over the top and serve with the rice.

**nutrition per serve**   Energy **2525 kJ (603 Cal)** Fat **38.6 g** Saturated fat **12.6 g**
Protein **45.7 g** Carbohydrate **19 g** Fibre **0.5 g** Cholesterol **245 mg** Sodium **257 g**

# Roast chicken with stuffing

**1.5 kg (3 lb 5 oz) whole chicken**

**2 tsp canola or olive oil**

**1 tbsp golden syrup or honey**

**Pumpkin and breadcrumb
   stuffing**

**10 g (¼ oz) butter**

**2 spring onions (scallions), thinly
   sliced**

**1 garlic clove, crushed**

**80 g (2¾ oz/1 cup) fresh gluten-free
   breadcrumbs**

**60 g (2¼ oz/1/2 cup) finely grated
   butternut pumpkin (squash)**

**Prep time** 30 minutes
**Cooking time** 1½ hours
**Serves** 4

**1**  Preheat the oven to 180°C (350°F/Gas 4). Lightly oil a roasting tin. To prepare the chicken, remove the neck, rinse out the cavity with cold water and pat dry with paper towels.

**2**  To make the stuffing, melt the butter in a small frying pan over medium heat, add the spring onions and garlic and cook, stirring, until softened. Combine the breadcrumbs and pumpkin in a bowl. Add the spring onion mixture and season with salt and pepper. Spoon the stuffing into the chicken cavity. Close the cavity using poultry pins or by tying the legs together with string. Tuck the neck flap underneath.

**3**  Combine the oil and golden syrup or honey in a small saucepan and heat until warm, then brush all over the chicken. Sprinkle lightly with salt and pepper.

**4**  Put the chicken in the roasting tin and roast for 1¼–1½ hours, basting every 15 minutes with the pan juices. Cover with oiled foil if the chicken starts to over-brown. It is cooked when the juices run clear when a skewer is inserted into the thickest part of the thigh. Rest for 10 minutes before carving.

# Fresh tomato and olive pasta

750 g (1 lb 10 oz) vine-ripened tomatoes, finely chopped

1 small red onion, finely chopped

2 garlic cloves, finely chopped

110 g (3½ oz/½ cup) chopped pitted green olives in brine

3 tbsp capers, rinsed, drained and chopped

1 tsp dried oregano

3 tbsp olive oil

1 tbsp white wine vinegar

500 g (1 lb 2 oz) gluten-free rigatoni

300 g (10½ oz) tin butter beans GF, drained and rinsed

1 handful oregano

**1**   Combine the tomatoes, onion, garlic, olives, capers and dried oregano in a bowl. Whisk together the oil and vinegar in a small bowl, then toss through the tomato mixture. Season with salt and pepper. Cover and set aside for at least 1 hour to allow the flavours to develop.

**2**   Meanwhile, cook the pasta in a large saucepan of boiling salted water for 10 minutes, or according to the packet instructions, until just tender. Drain and return to the saucepan. Toss the tomato mixture and butter beans through the hot pasta. Divide among four bowls, then garnish with the oregano leaves.

**Prep time** 15 minutes +
1 hour standing
**Cooking time** 10 minutes
**Serves** 4

**nutrition per serve (6)**  Energy **1454 kJ (346 Cal)**  Fat **13.2 g**  Saturated fat **1.8 g**
Protein **33.4 g**  Carbohydrate **21.7 g**  Fibre **3.9 g**  Cholesterol **363 mg**  Sodium **494 g**

# Greek-style calamari

**Stuffing**

2 tsp olive oil

2 spring onions (scallions), sliced

280 g (10 oz/1½ cups) cold, cooked
  basmati rice

4 tbsp pine nuts

4 tbsp finely chopped dried apricots

2 tbsp chopped parsley

2 tsp finely grated lemon zest

1 egg, lightly beaten

1 kg (2 lb 4 oz) cleaned squid tubes

**Sauce**

4 large ripe tomatoes

2 tsp olive oil

1 onion, finely chopped

1 garlic clove, crushed

3 tbsp good-quality red wine

1 tbsp chopped oregano

**Prep time** 30 minutes
**Cooking time** 35 minutes
**Serves** 4–6

**1**  Preheat the oven to 160°C (315°F/Gas 2–3). To make
the stuffing, mix together the oil, spring onion, rice,
pine nuts, apricots, parsley and lemon zest in a bowl.
Add enough egg to moisten all the ingredients.

**2**  Wash the squid tubes and pat dry inside and out with
paper towels. Three-quarters fill each squid tube with
the stuffing. Secure the ends with toothpicks or
skewers. Place in a single layer in a casserole dish.

**3**  To make the sauce, begin by peeling the tomatoes.
Score a cross in the base of each one. Cover with boiling
water for 30 seconds, then plunge into cold water. Drain
and peel away the tomato skin from the cross. Chop the
flesh. Heat the oil in a frying pan. Add the onion and
garlic and cook over low heat for 2 minutes, or until the
onion is soft. Add the tomato, wine and oregano and
bring to the boil. Reduce the heat, cover with a lid and
cook over low heat for 10 minutes.

**4**  Pour the hot sauce over the squid, cover and bake for
20 minutes, or until the squid is tender. Remove the
toothpicks before cutting into thick slices for serving.
Spoon the sauce over just before serving.

**nutrition per serve**   Energy **2058 kJ (492 Cal)**  Fat **9.1 g**  Saturated fat **2.4 g**
Protein **42.7 g**  Carbohydrate **56.1 g**  Fibre **4 g**  Cholesterol **188 mg**  Sodium **450 g**

# Rice-crumbed fish with wedges

2 eggs

2 tbsp milk

4 tbsp gluten-free plain (all-purpose) flour

80 g (2¾ oz/1 cup) rice crumbs

4 boneless white fish fillets

canola or olive oil spray

lettuce or salad leaves, to serve

chutney ᴳᶠ (Basics), to serve

**Wedges**

1 kg (2 lb 4 oz) all-purpose potatoes, peeled and cut into wedges

canola or olive oil spray

**Prep time** 20 minutes
**Cooking time** 50 minutes
**Serves** 4

**1**  Preheat the oven to 220°C (425°F/Gas 7). Line two large baking trays with sheets of baking paper.

**2**  Combine the eggs and milk in a shallow bowl. Put the flour in a shallow dish and season with salt and pepper. Put the rice crumbs in a separate shallow dish. Dip the fish in the flour, followed by the egg mixture and, lastly, the rice crumbs. Lay the crumbed fish in a single layer on one of the lined trays. Refrigerate until required.

**3**  Put the potato wedges in a large bowl and sprinkle with salt. Spray the wedges with oil, then toss to coat. Spread over the second lined tray.

**4**  Bake the potato wedges for 30 minutes, turning once. Put the wedges on the lower shelf of the oven. Remove the fish from the fridge, then spray both sides of the fish lightly with oil. Add the fish to the top shelf and cook for 20 minutes, or until the fish is cooked and the wedges are crispy. Serve the fish with the wedges, lettuce and chutney.

nutrition per serve   Energy **1170 kJ (279 Cal)**  Fat **8.1 g**  Saturated fat **1.8 g**
Protein **42.2 g**  Carbohydrate **6 g**  Fibre **1.1 g**  Cholesterol **122 mg**  Sodium **715 g**

# Fish steaks with mushrooms

**2 tbsp tamari** GF

**1 tbsp canola or olive oil**

**grated zest and juice of 1 lemon**

**2 tbsp Chinese rice wine or
dry sherry**

**4 x 200 g (7 oz) snapper steaks**

**1 tsp sesame oil**

**150 g (5½ oz) fresh shiitake
mushrooms, sliced**

**2 spring onions (scallions), sliced**

**Prep time** 15 minutes +
4 hours marinating
**Cooking time** 35 minutes
Serves 4

**1**   Mix the tamari, oil, lemon zest and juice and rice wine
or sherry together in a bowl. Put the fish steaks in a
shallow, glass or ceramic ovenproof dish in which they
fit snugly in a single layer. Pour the marinade over the
fish and turn them once so both sides are coated. Cover
and refrigerate for at least 4 hours, or overnight, turning
the fish over in the marinade a couple of times.

**2**   Remove the fish from the fridge and let it return
to room temperature. Preheat the oven to 180°C
(350°F/Gas 4).

**3**   Heat the sesame oil in a frying pan over medium heat
and, when hot, add the mushrooms. Cook and stir for
3–4 minutes, or until starting to soften. Add the spring
onions, then stir and remove the pan from the heat.

**4**   Sprinkle the mushroom and onion mixture over the fish
and bake, covered with a lid or foil, for 25–30 minutes,
or until the fish is opaque and firm to the touch.

# Chicken with baked eggplant

1 red capsicum (pepper)

1 eggplant (aubergine)

3 tomatoes

200 g (7 oz) large button mushrooms

1 onion

canola or olive oil spray

1½ tbsp tomato paste (concentrated purée) GF

125 ml (4 fl oz/½ cup) chicken stock GF (Basics)

3 tbsp dry white wine

2 low-fat bacon slices GF

4 boneless, skinless chicken breasts

4 small sprigs of rosemary

Prep time 30 minutes

Cooking time 1½ hours

Serves 4

1   Preheat the oven to 200°C (400°F/Gas 6). Cut the capsicum and eggplant into bite-sized pieces. Cut the tomatoes into quarters, the mushrooms in half and the onion into thin wedges. Mix the vegetables together in a roasting tin. Spray with the oil and bake for 1 hour, or until starting to brown and soften, stirring once.

2   Mix together the tomato paste, stock and wine, then pour into the roasting tin and roast the vegetables for a further 10 minutes, or until the sauce has thickened.

3   Meanwhile, cut bacon in half lengthways. Wrap a strip around each chicken breast and secure it underneath with a toothpick. Poke a sprig of fresh rosemary underneath the bacon. Heat a non-stick frying pan over medium heat. Spray with the oil. Cook the chicken for 2–3 minutes on each side, or until golden on both sides. Cover and cook for 10–15 minutes, or until the chicken is cooked through. Remove the toothpicks. Serve the chicken on a bed of the vegetables.

# Pork and cabbage noodle stir-fry

**Sauce**

1½ tbsp fish sauce GF

4 tbsp tamari GF

1½ tbsp grated palm sugar or soft
   brown sugar

375 g (13 oz) thin rice stick noodles

2 tsp canola or olive oil

1 onion, finely chopped

2 garlic cloves, finely chopped

1–2 long red chillies, seeded and
   finely chopped

500 g (1 lb 2 oz) lean minced
   (ground) pork

1 large carrot, peeled and grated

1 zucchini (courgette), grated

225 g (8 oz/3 cups) thinly shredded
   cabbage

1 large handful coriander (cilantro)
   leaves

**1** Combine the sauce ingredients in a small bowl, stirring
to dissolve the sugar. Place the noodles in a large bowl
and cover with boiling water. Set aside for 4 minutes, or
until softened. Drain well. Use scissors to cut the
noodles into shorter lengths.

**2** Heat the oil in a wok. Add the onion, garlic, chilli and
pork and stir-fry for 4 minutes, or until browned and
cooked. Break up any lumps as you cook.

**3** Stir in the carrot, zucchini and cabbage and continue
to stir-fry for a further 2–3 minutes, or until the
vegetables are just cooked. Stir through the noodles,
then the sauce ingredients and coriander leaves.

**Prep time** 15 minutes
**Cooking time** 10 minutes
**Serves** 4

nutrition per serve (8)  Energy **1782 kJ (426 Cal)** Fat **14.3 g** Saturated fat **6.6 g**
Protein **26 g** Carbohydrate **49 g** Fibre **4.2 g** Cholesterol **57 mg** Sodium **400 g**

# Beef and spinach lasagne

1 tbsp canola or olive oil

1 large onion, finely chopped

3 large garlic cloves, crushed

1 celery stalk, diced

500 g (1 lb 2 oz) lean minced
(ground) beef

1 tsp dried oregano

2 x 400 g (14 oz) tins diced tomatoes

2 tbsp tomato paste (concentrated
purée) GF

250 ml (9 fl oz/1 cup) beef stock GF
(Basics) or water

500 g (1 lb 2 oz/1 bunch) English
spinach, stalks removed, washed

375 g (13 oz) gluten-free lasagne
sheets

White sauce

3 tbsp pure maize cornflour
(cornstarch) GF

375 ml (13 fl oz/1½ cups) reduced-
fat milk

1 slice of onion

½ tsp ground nutmeg

150 g (5½ oz/⅔ cup) ricotta cheese

90 g (3¼ oz/¾ cup firmly packed)
grated cheddar cheese GF

**1**  Heat oil in a large, non-stick saucepan. Add onion and cook for 2 minutes. Add garlic and celery and cook for a further 2 minutes. Add beef and oregano and cook over high heat for 5 minutes, breaking up any lumps with a spoon. Add tomatoes, tomato paste and stock or water and season with salt and pepper. Reduce heat to low and simmer, covered, for 1 hour until reduced and thickened, stirring occasionally. If sauce is too thin, remove lid and simmer until reduced and thickened. Cool slightly. Cook spinach with just the water clinging to leaves in a covered saucepan for 1 minute.

**2**  Meanwhile, to make the white sauce, put cornflour in a saucepan, add a little of the milk and mix to a smooth paste. Add remaining milk, onion slice and nutmeg. Stir constantly over medium heat until sauce boils and thickens. Reduce heat and simmer for 1 minute. Remove onion. Stir in cheeses, then mix until smooth.

**3**  Preheat oven to 180°C (350°F/Gas 4). Arrange one-third of the lasagne sheets over the base of a 4 litre (140 fl oz/16 cup) rectangular ovenproof dish. Spoon over half the beef, then cover with half the spinach. Cover with another layer of pasta and spoon over remaining beef. Cover with remaining spinach, then remaining pasta. Spread over the white sauce. Bake for 30 minutes, or until golden. Rest for 5 minutes before slicing.

**Prep time** 30 minutes
**Cooking time** 1¾ hours
**Serves** 6–8

nutrition per serve   Energy **1892 kJ (451 Cal)**  Fat **20 g**  Saturated fat **5.5 g**
Protein **34.6 g**  Carbohydrate **31.1 g**  Fibre **7.2 g**  Cholesterol **78 mg**  Sodium **345 g**

# Greek-style lamb

**400 g (14 oz) lean lamb fillets**

**1 tsp olive oil**

**1 large red onion, sliced**

**3 zucchini (courgettes), thinly sliced**

**200 g (7 oz) cherry tomatoes, halved**

**3 garlic cloves, crushed**

**60 g (2¼ oz/½ cup) pitted black olives in brine, drained and halved**

**2 tbsp lemon juice**

**2 tbsp oregano**

**100 g (3½ oz/⅔ cup) crumbled low-fat feta cheese**

**4 tbsp pine nuts, lightly toasted**

**Prep time** 20 minutes

**Cooking time** 10 minutes

**Serves** 4

**1** Trim the lamb, then cut across the grain into thin strips. Heat a large frying pan until hot and lightly brush with oil. Add the lamb in small batches and cook each batch over high heat for 1–2 minutes, or until browned. Remove all the lamb from the pan.

**2** Heat the oil in the pan, then add the onion and zucchini. Cook, stirring, over high heat for 2 minutes, or until just tender. Add the cherry tomatoes and garlic. Cook for 1–2 minutes, or until the tomatoes have just softened. Return the meat to the pan and stir over high heat until heated through.

**3** Remove the pan from the heat. Add the olives, lemon juice and oregano and toss until well combined. Sprinkle with crumbled feta cheese and pine nuts before serving.

# Thai chicken salad

100 g (3½ oz) dried rice vermicelli

250 g (9 oz) minced (ground) chicken

200 g (7 oz) tin water chestnuts, drained and chopped

2 tbsp fish sauce <sup>GF</sup>

2 tbsp lime juice

1 lemon grass stem, white part only, finely chopped

3 spring onions (scallions), thinly sliced

3 tbsp chopped Thai basil

3 tbsp chopped mint

**Prep time** 15 minutes +
10 minutes soaking
**Cooking time** 5 minutes
Serves 4

**1**  Put the dried rice vermicelli in a large bowl. Pour over enough boiling water to cover and soak for 10 minutes, or until tender. Drain and pat dry.

**2**  Put the chicken, water chestnuts, fish sauce, lime juice, lemon grass and 3 tablespoons water in a frying pan and stir over medium heat for 5 minutes, or until the chicken is cooked. Set aside to cool. Transfer to a bowl and add the spring onions, basil, mint and vermicelli. Toss well to combine. Serve immediately.

**nutrition per serve**  Energy **1736 kJ (415 Cal)** Fat **8.9 g** Saturated fat **3.5 g**
Protein **29.7 g** Carbohydrate **51.7 g** Fibre **3 g** Cholesterol **72 mg** Sodium **1365 g**

# Beef and noodle salad

**Dressing**

2 tbsp finely chopped lemongrass,
    white part only

1 small red chilli

3 tbsp tamari <sup>GF</sup>

3 tbsp lime juice

1 tbsp fish sauce <sup>GF</sup>

1 tbsp grated palm sugar or soft
    brown sugar

1 tsp grated fresh ginger


500 g (1 lb 2 oz) lean sirloin steak

200 g (7 oz) cellophane (bean thread)
    noodles

1 Lebanese (short) cucumber

1 small red onion

4 ripe Roma (plum) tomatoes

1 tbsp thinly shredded fresh ginger

90 g (3¼ oz/1 cup) bean sprouts,
    trimmed

1 handful mint, torn

1 handful basil, torn

1 handful coriander (cilantro) leaves

**1**  Bruise the lemongrass using a mortar and pestle or a heavy object such as a rolling pin. Seed and finely chop the chilli. Combine the dressing ingredients using a mortar and pestle or in a bowl and stir to dissolve the sugar. Put 1 tablespoon of the dressing in a shallow non-metallic dish with the meat. Coat the meat with the dressing and marinate for at least 15 minutes. Set aside the remaining dressing.

**2**  Spray a non-stick frying pan or chargrill pan with oil. Heat the oil until very hot. Add the steak and cook for 2–3 minutes on each side, or until cooked as desired. Remove and set aside for 5 minutes, then slice thinly.

**3**  Place the noodles in a large bowl and cover with boiling water. Set aside for 4 minutes, drain well and refresh under cold water. Use scissors to cut into short lengths.

**4**  Cut the cucumber in half lengthways, then thinly slice on the diagonal. Cut the onion into thin wedges. Cut the tomatoes into quarters. Put into a large bowl with the rest of the ingredients. Toss together gently with the remaining dressing so everything is covered. Serve immediately.

**Prep time** 15 minutes +
15 minutes marinating
**Cooking time** 10 minutes
**Serves** 4

**nutrition per serve** Energy **2580 kJ (616 Cal)** Fat **5.8 g** Saturated fat **1.4 g**
Protein **40.6 g** Carbohydrate **92.6 g** Fibre **1.3 g** Cholesterol **233 mg** Sodium **1522 g**

# Seafood risotto

12 black mussels

125 ml (4 fl oz/½ cup) dry white
wine

1.5 litres (52 fl oz/6 cups) fish or
chicken stock <sup>GF</sup> (Basics)

1 small pinch of saffron threads

2 tsp olive oil

8 raw prawns (shrimp), peeled and
deveined, tails intact

8 scallops, trimmed with coral intact

3 small squid tubes, cleaned and cut
into rings

1 onion, finely chopped

2 garlic cloves, crushed

440 g (15½ oz/2 cups) arborio rice

2 tbsp chopped flat-leaf (Italian)
parsley

Prep time 25 minutes
Cooking time 45 minutes
Serves 4

**1** Scrub the mussels with a stiff brush and remove the beards. Discard any broken mussels or any that don't close when tapped. Place the mussels in a heavy-based saucepan with the wine and cook, covered, over high heat, for 3–4 minutes, or until the mussels have just opened. Remove any that have not opened and discard. Strain and reserve the liquid and set the mussels aside.

**2** Combine the mussel liquid, stock and saffron in a saucepan, then cover and keep at a low simmer. Heat 1 teaspoon of the oil in a non-stick frying pan over medium–high heat. Add the prawns and cook until they just turn pink. Remove to a plate, then cook the scallops and squid in batches for 1–2 minutes, or until lightly golden. Remove and set aside with the mussels and prawns.

**3** Heat the remaining teaspoon of oil in a heavy-based saucepan, then add the onion and garlic. Reduce the heat to low and cook for 5–6 minutes, or until soft and translucent. Add the rice and stir until coated. Add 125 ml (4 fl oz/½ cup) of the hot stock, stirring constantly with a wooden spoon until absorbed. Continue adding 125 ml (4 fl oz/½ cup) of liquid at a time, stirring constantly, until all the liquid is absorbed. This should take about 25 minutes. Stir through the seafood and parsley. Season to taste and serve immediately.

# Hamburgers

**500 g (1 lb 2 oz) lean minced (ground) beef**

**4 spring onions (scallions), thinly sliced**

**3 tbsp snipped chives**

**1 garlic clove, crushed**

**1 egg**

**25 g (1 oz/1¼ cups) gluten-free puffed rice, finely crushed**

**canola or olive oil, for frying**

**6 gluten-free bread rolls**

**40 g (1½ oz) butter**

**½ head lettuce**

**chutney GF or tomato sauce GF (Basics)**

**1**   Combine beef, spring onions, chives, garlic, egg, puffed rice and 3 tablespoons water in a large bowl. Season with salt and pepper. Using your hands, knead mixture until well combined. Divide mixture into six portions. Roll into balls, then flatten into patties. Heat oil in a large frying pan over medium heat, add patties and cook for about 4–6 minutes on each side, or until cooked through and lightly browned.

**2**   Butter the buns and grill (broil), for 1–2 minutes, or until crisp and golden brown.

**3**   Place a patty and lettuce into bread roll. Serve topped with a dollop of chutney or tomato sauce. For extra flavour, serve with cooked onions.

**Prep time** 30 minutes
**Cooking time** 20 minutes
**Makes** 6

# Desserts

# Baked raisin apples

**4 cooking apples**

**80 g (2¾ oz/⅓ cup firmly packed) soft brown sugar**

**1½ tbsp chopped raisins**

**½ tsp ground cinnamon (optional)**

**20 g (¾ oz) unsalted butter**

**low-fat plain yoghurt or ricotta cream, to serve**

**Prep time** 10 minutes

**Cooking time** 35 minutes

**Serves** 4

**1** Preheat the oven to 220°C (425°F/Gas 7). Use an apple corer to remove the core of the apples, then score the skin around the middle.

**2** Combine the sugar, raisins and cinnamon in a bowl. Place each apple on a piece of heavy-duty foil and stuff it with the filling. Spread a little butter over the top of each apple, then wrap the foil securely around the apples. Bake for about 35 minutes, or until cooked. Serve with yoghurt or ricotta cream.

# Chocolate self-saucing pudding

150 g (5½ oz/1¼ cups) soy-containing, gluten-free
   self-raising flour

1 tsp gluten-free baking powder

80 g (2¾ oz/⅓ cup firmly packed) soft brown sugar

125 ml (4 fl oz/½ cup) milk

2 tbsp pure unsweetened cocoa powder ᴳꟳ

60 g (2¼ oz) unsalted butter, melted, cooled

1 egg, lightly beaten

165 g (5¾ oz/¾ cup firmly packed) soft brown sugar, extra

2 tbsp pure unsweetened cocoa powder ᴳꟳ, extra

**Prep time** 20 minutes

**Cooking time** 45 minutes

**Serves** 4–6

**1**  Preheat the oven to 170°C (325°F/Gas 3). Lightly grease
a 1.25 litre (44 fl oz/5 cup) capacity ovenproof dish.

**2**  Sift the flour and baking powder into a large bowl and
add the sugar; make a well in the centre. In a separate
bowl, whisk the milk and cocoa powder together until
smooth. Set aside to cool. Add the butter and egg to the
cocoa mixture and whisk to combine. Pour into the well
in the flour mixture and whisk until a smooth, thick
batter forms. Pour into the prepared dish. Place the dish
on a baking tray.

**3**  Sprinkle the extra brown sugar over the batter. Whisk
375 ml (13 fl oz/1½ cups) boiling water and the extra
cocoa powder together until smooth. Carefully pour
over the batter. Bake for 35–45 minutes, or until a
skewer inserted halfway into the pudding comes out
clean. Serve immediately. As a treat, top with cream.

nutrition per serve   Energy **382 kJ (91 Cal)** Fat **0.2 g** Saturated fat **0 g**
Protein **4.5 g** Carbohydrate **18.8 g** Fibre **3 g** Cholesterol **0 mg** Sodium **23 g**

# Apple snow

**4 green apples, peeled, cored and
    chopped**

**1 tsp sugar**

**½ tsp ground cinnamon**

**2 tsp powdered gelatine**

**3 egg whites**

**Prep time** 10 minutes +
30 minutes refrigeration
**Cooking time** 10 minutes
**Serves** 4

**1**  Put the chopped apples, sugar, cinnamon and
3 tablespoons water in a saucepan. Simmer, covered,
for 8 minutes, or until tender. Mash until puréed.

**2**  Sprinkle the gelatine over 1 tablespoon of water in a
small heatproof bowl and leave to go spongy. Put the
bowl in a saucepan of just boiled water, off the heat
(the water should come halfway up the bowl). Stir to
dissolve. Stir into the hot purée.

**3**  Beat the egg whites until stiff peaks form, then fold into
the hot purée—the heat should slightly cook the whites.
Spoon the mixture into glass bowls or parfait glasses,
then refrigerate for at least 30 minutes before serving.

# Lemongrass and ginger fruit salad

**3 tbsp caster (superfine) sugar**

**2 x 2 cm (¾ x ¾ in) piece of fresh ginger, thinly sliced**

**1 lemongrass stem, bruised and halved**

**pulp from 1 large passionfruit**

**1 Fiji red pawpaw**

**½ honeydew melon**

**1 large mango**

**1 small pineapple**

**12 lychees**

**1 large handful mint, shredded, to serve**

1  Place the sugar, ginger and lemongrass in a small saucepan, add 125 ml (4 fl oz/½ cup) water and stir over low heat to dissolve the sugar. Boil for 5 minutes, or until reduced to 4 tablespoons, then set aside to cool. Strain the syrup and add the passionfruit pulp.

2  Peel and seed the pawpaw and melon. Cut the pawpaw and the melon into 4 cm (1½ in) cubes. Peel the mango and cut the flesh into cubes, discarding the stone. Peel, halve and core the pineapple and cut into cubes. Peel the lychees, then make a slit in the flesh and remove the seed.

3  Place all the fruit in a large serving bowl. Pour the syrup over the fruit, or serve separately, if you prefer. Garnish with the mint.

**Prep time** 20 minutes

**Cooking time** 10 minutes

**Serves** 4

nutrition per serve (6)   Energy **1079 kJ (257 Cal)** Fat **0.3 g** Saturated fat **0.2 g**
Protein **6.6 g** Carbohydrate **57.9 g** Fibre **1.6 g** Cholesterol **4 mg** Sodium **76 g**

# Creamed rice with apricots

**24 dried apricot halves**

**750 ml (26 fl oz/3 cups) skim milk**

**110 g (3¾ oz/½ cup) arborio rice**

**1 vanilla bean, split lengthways**

**¼ tsp ground nutmeg**

**pinch of ground cardamom**

**2 tsp caster (superfine) sugar**

**165 g (5¾ oz/¾ cup) sugar**

**2 cinnamon sticks**

**2 tsp grated orange zest**

**3 tbsp orange juice**

**Prep time** 10 minutes +
30 minutes soaking
**Cooking time** 50 minutes
**Serves** 4–6

**1**  Put the apricots in a heatproof bowl, cover with boiling water and leave to soak for 30 minutes, or until the apricots are plump.

**2**  Pour the milk into a saucepan, add the rice, vanilla bean, nutmeg and cardamom and bring to the boil. Reduce the heat and simmer gently, stirring frequently, for 25 minutes, or until the rice is soft and creamy and has absorbed most of the milk. Remove from the heat.

**3**  Remove the vanilla bean, scrape out the seeds with the tip of a knife and mix them into the rice. Stir in the caster sugar.

**4**  Meanwhile, to make the sugar syrup, put the sugar, cinnamon sticks, orange zest and juice in a saucepan with 625 ml (21½ fl oz/2½ cups) water. Bring to the boil, then reduce the heat and simmer for 10 minutes. Drain the apricots and add to the pan. Return to the boil, then reduce the heat to low and simmer for 5 minutes, or until soft. Remove the apricots with a slotted spoon. Return the sauce to the boil, then boil until reduced by half. Remove from the heat, cool a little and pour over the apricots. Serve the apricots with the creamed rice.

nutrition per serve   Energy **320 kJ (76 Cal)**   Fat **0.05 g**   Saturated fat **0 g**
Protein **2.4 g**   Carbohydrate **16.3 g**   Fibre **4 g**   Cholesterol **0 mg**   Sodium **31 g**

# Passionfruit sorbet

**400 g (14 oz) tin peach slices in natural juice**

**400 g (14 oz) tin pear halves in natural juice**

**3 tbsp caster (superfine) sugar**

**4 tbsp fresh passionfruit pulp**

**1 tbsp lemon juice**

**2 egg whites**

**fresh fruit, to serve**

**Prep time** 15 minutes + freezing

**Cooking time** Nil

**Serves** 6

**1** Drain the tinned fruit and reserve the juice. Put the reserved juice and sugar in a small saucepan. Stir over low heat for 2 minutes until the sugar has dissolved. Cool.

**2** Strain the passionfruit pulp into a small bowl, reserving the seeds. Put the strained passionfruit juice, the drained tinned fruit, the cooled fruit juice and lemon juice in a food processor. Blend until smooth. Stir in the reserved passionfruit seeds.

**3** Pour into a shallow 27 x 17 cm (10¾ x 6½ in) tin and freeze for 3 hours, stirring occasionally, until the mixture is icy. Use a fork to roughly mash the mixture. Put in a bowl and beat with electric beaters until smooth and creamy looking.

**4** Beat the egg whites until firm peaks form, then fold into the creamed fruit mixture until just combined. Do not over-mix. Spoon into a 1.5 litre (52 fl oz/6 cup) loaf (bar) tin. Cover with plastic wrap and freeze until firm.

**5** To serve, put tin in the refrigerator for about 15 minutes to allow the sorbet to soften a little. Use an ice-cream scoop and serve 2–3 scoops of sorbet per person. Serve with fruit.

nutrition per serve   Energy **1708 kJ (408 Cal)** Fat **11.1 g** Saturated fat **6.5 g**
Protein **4.8 g** Carbohydrate **72.8 g** Fibre **1.9 g** Cholesterol **61 mg** Sodium **526 g**

# Butterscotch pudding

190 g (6¾ oz/1¼ cups) gluten-free
self-raising flour

1 tsp gluten-free baking powder

80 g (2¾ oz/⅓ cup firmly packed)
soft brown sugar

170 ml (5½ fl oz/⅔ cup) milk

60 g (2¼ oz) unsalted butter, melted,
cooled

1 egg

1 tbsp golden syrup or pure maple
syrup

165 g (5¾ oz/¾ cup firmly packed)
soft brown sugar, extra

2 tbsp golden syrup or pure maple
syrup, extra

**Prep time** 20 minutes

**Cooking time** 45 minutes

**Serves** 4–6

**1** Preheat the oven to 170°C (325°F/Gas 3). Lightly grease a 1.25 litre (44 fl oz/5 cup) ovenproof dish.

**2** Sift the flour and baking powder into a large bowl. Stir in the sugar, then make a well in the centre. In a separate bowl, whisk milk, butter, egg and golden syrup or maple syrup together. Pour into the well in the dry ingredients and whisk until a smooth batter forms. Pour into prepared dish. Place the dish on a baking tray.

**3** Sprinkle the extra brown sugar over the batter. Combine the extra golden syrup or maple syrup and 420 ml (14½ fl oz/1⅔ cups) boiling water and carefully pour over the batter. Bake the pudding for 35–45 minutes, or until a skewer inserted halfway into the pudding comes out clean.

**4** Set the pudding aside for 5–10 minutes to allow the sauce to thicken slightly before serving.

# Peaches with ricotta cream

**4 large peaches, unpeeled**

**500 ml (17 fl oz/2 cups) unsweetened apple juice**

**1 tbsp caster (superfine) sugar**

**2 tsp lemon juice**

**3 tbsp flaked almonds, lightly toasted**

**Ricotta Cream**

**200 g (7 oz) low-fat ricotta cheese**

**1 tsp caster (superfine) sugar**

**1 tsp natural vanilla extract**

**1 tsp grated lemon zest**

**Prep time** 20 minutes
**Cooking time** 10 minutes
**Serves** 4

**1**  Cut the peaches in half and remove the stone. Heat the apple juice in a saucepan over medium heat, then add the sugar and lemon juice and stir until dissolved. Add the peach halves and poach, covered, over low heat for 5–8 minutes, or until just tender when pierced with a knife. Remove with a slotted spoon and peel away the skins. Cool. Reserve the poaching juice.

**2**  To make the ricotta cream, put the ricotta, sugar, vanilla and lemon zest in a bowl and beat with electric beaters until smooth. Cover with plastic wrap, then refrigerate to firm.

**3**  Serve the peach halves with a little of the reserved juice, then spoon over the ricotta cream and sprinkle with the almonds.

# Crêpes with coffee sauce

**Coffee Sauce**

**2 tbsp golden syrup or pure maple syrup**

**3 tsp instant coffee powder**

**2 tbsp pure maize cornflour (cornstarch) GF**

**235 g (8½ oz/1 cup firmly packed) soft brown sugar**

**Crêpes**

**190 g (6¾ oz/1¼ cups) gluten-free plain (all-purpose) flour**

**2 tsp gluten-free baking powder**

**1 egg**

**2 tbsp canola oil**

**Prep time** 35 minutes

**Cooking time** 25 minutes

**Makes** 10

**1**  To make the coffee sauce, combine the syrup, coffee powder, cornflour and sugar in a frying pan. Add 250 ml (9 fl oz/1 cup) water and blend. Put the pan over medium heat. Stir constantly until the mixture boils and thickens. Reduce the heat and simmer for 2–3 minutes. Set aside.

**2**  To make the crêpes, sift the flour and baking powder into a bowl. Gradually add the combined egg, 1 tablespoon of the oil and 310 ml (10¾ fl oz/1¼ cups) water, stirring well until the batter is smooth and the consistency of thin cream, adding more water if needed. Strain into a vessel with a pouring lip.

**3**  Lightly brush a 20 cm (8 in) frying pan with a little of the remaining oil and heat over medium heat. Pour in just enough crêpe batter to thinly cover the bottom of the pan. When the top of the crêpe starts to set, turn it over with a spatula. After browning the second side, transfer to a plate. Repeat with the remaining crêpe batter, greasing the pan between each. Fold each crêpe in four to form a triangle.

**4**  Reheat the sauce in a frying pan over low heat. Put the crêpes in the pan and heat gently until warmed through. Place the crêpes on two serving plates and spoon any extra warm sauce over the top.

# Strawberry and raspberry parfait

**85 g (3 oz) packet diet strawberry-flavoured jelly (gelatin dessert) crystals**

**250 g (9 oz/1²⁄₃ cups) strawberries, hulled**

**500 g (1 lb 2 oz) low-fat vanilla ice cream ᴳᶠ**

**125 g (4¹⁄₂ oz/1 cup) raspberries**

**Prep time** 10 minutes +
1 hour setting
**Cooking time** Nil
**Serves** 6

**1**  Put the jelly crystals in a heatproof bowl and pour over 250 ml (9 fl oz/1 cup) boiling water. Stir to dissolve the crystals, then add 250 ml (9 fl oz/1 cup) cold water. Put the bowl in refrigerator for at least 1 hour, or until set.

**2**  Process the strawberries in a food processor for 15 seconds until blended to a pulp.

**3**  Layer the jelly, strawberry purée and ice cream into six parfait glasses. Top with raspberries, then serve immediately.

nutrition per serve   Energy 1227 kJ (293 Cal)  Fat 0.2 g  Saturated fat 0.02 g
Protein 1.8 g  Carbohydrate 72 g  Fibre 3.7 g  Cholesterol 1 mg  Sodium 23 g

# Poached pears in vanilla syrup

170 g (6 oz/¾ cup) caster (superfine)
   sugar

1 vanilla bean, split lengthways and
   scraped

1 strip lemon zest

1½ tsp lemongrass tea leaves

4 large firm pears, peeled, with stems
   intact

4 tbsp low-fat plain yoghurt

Prep time 15 minutes
Cooking time 50 minutes
Serves 4

1   Put the sugar, vanilla bean and lemon zest in a large
    saucepan with 500 ml (17 fl oz/2 cups) water. Put the
    lemongrass in a tea-infuser ball or small muslin
    (cheesecloth) bag, and add to the saucepan. Heat over
    low heat, stirring occasionally, until the sugar melts.

2   Bring to the boil, then reduce to a simmer and add the
    pears, laying them on their sides. Cover and simmer,
    turning occasionally, for 30 minutes, or until the pears
    are tender when pierced with a skewer.

3   Remove the pears with a slotted spoon and set aside to
    cool. Meanwhile, increase the heat to high and simmer
    the syrup for 8–10 minutes, or until reduced by half and
    thickened slightly. Remove the vanilla bean, lemon zest
    and lemongrass tea. Serve the pears drizzled with the
    syrup and a dollop of the yoghurt on the side.

# Apple sago pudding

4 tbsp caster (superfine) sugar

100 g (3½ oz/½ cup) sago

600 ml (21 fl oz) milk

4 tbsp sultanas (golden raisins)

1 tsp natural vanilla extract

pinch of ground nutmeg

¼ tsp ground cinnamon

2 eggs, lightly beaten

3 small ripe apples (about 250 g/9 oz), peeled,
cored and very thinly sliced

1 tbsp soft brown sugar

**1**   Preheat the oven to 180°C (350°F/Gas 4). Grease a
1.5 litre (52 fl oz/6 cup) ceramic soufflé dish. Place the
sugar, sago, milk and sultanas in a saucepan. Heat the
mixture, stirring often. Bring to the boil, then reduce
the heat and simmer for 5 minutes.

**2**   Stir in the vanilla extract, nutmeg, cinnamon, egg and
the apple slices, then pour the mixture into the
prepared dish. Sprinkle with the brown sugar and bake
for 45 minutes, or until set and golden brown.

**Prep time** 15 minutes
**Cooking time** 50 minutes
**Serves** 4

**nutrition per serve (8)**   Energy **1081 kJ** (258 Cal)  Fat **10.1 g**  Saturated fat **6.3 g**
Protein **1.8 g**  Carbohydrate **39.8 g**  Fibre **1.7 g**  Cholesterol **52 mg**  Sodium **412 g**

# Apple and berry pie

400 g (14 oz) tin pie (baker's) apples GF

3 tbsp caster (superfine) sugar

1 tsp grated lemon zest

1 tbsp polenta

1 quantity gluten-free sweet shortcrust pastry (Basics)

165 g (5¾ oz/1½ cups) mixed fresh or frozen berries

raw (demerara) sugar, to sprinkle

**Prep time** 30 minutes + chilling
**Cooking time** 45 minutes
**Serves** 6–8

1  Preheat the oven to 200°C (400°F/Gas 6). Lightly grease a pie dish or pie tin that is 18 cm (7 in) across the base. Put the apples, caster sugar, lemon zest and polenta in a bowl and stir to combine.

2  Roll the pastry between two sheets of baking paper to a rough 30 cm (12 in) circle. Carefully turn the pastry into the prepared dish with the pastry overlapping the edge of the dish.

3  Stir the berries through the apple mixture, then add the apple and berry mixture to the centre of the pastry. Fold over the overlapping edges leaving the fruit in the centre exposed. Sprinkle the pastry with raw sugar.

4  Put the dish on a baking tray. Bake for 35-45 minutes, or until the pastry is crisp and lightly browned. Cover with foil if browning too much. Serve hot or warm. For an indulgent dessert, serve with low fat cream.

# Baking

nutrition per slice (10)   Energy **1193 kJ (284 Cal)** Fat **14.8 g** Saturated fat **1.7 g**
Protein **4.4 g** Carbohydrate **33.1 g** Fibre **2 g** Cholesterol **56 mg** Sodium **953 g**

# Walnut and seed bread

3 eggs, lightly beaten

3 tbsp canola or olive oil

500 g (1 lb 2 oz/4 cups) soy-
  containing, gluten-free plain
  (all-purpose) flour

1 tsp soft brown sugar

2 tsp dried yeast GF

½ tsp salt

¼ tsp tartaric acid

1 tbsp each of sunflower seeds,
  pepitas and poppy seeds

85 g (3 oz/⅔ cup) chopped walnuts

canola or olive oil, extra, for glazing

mixed seeds, to sprinkle

**Prep time** 30 minutes +
50 minutes rising
**Cooking time** 45 minutes
**Serves** 8–10

1  Preheat the oven to 200°C (400°F/Gas 6). Lightly grease a 23 cm (9 in) round cake tin and line the base with baking paper.

2  Beat together the eggs, oil and 500 ml (17 fl oz/2 cups) warm water in a bowl. Put the flour, sugar, yeast, salt and tartaric acid in a separate large bowl. Using electric beaters, beat on a low speed for 20 seconds to combine. With the motor running, gradually beat in the egg mixture until smooth. Continue to beat for 5 minutes. Add the seeds and chopped walnuts and beat until incorporated.

3  Pour the batter into the prepared tin. Cover with greased plastic wrap and set aside in a warm place for 50 minutes until the batter has nearly risen to the top of the tin. Brush top of the loaf lightly with oil and sprinkle with the extra seeds. Bake for 45 minutes, or until  golden brown.

4  Cool in the tin for 10 minutes, then turn out onto a wire rack to cool completely. Cut into slices to serve. For the family, you may spread it with some butter.

# Cheese pinwheels

**120 g (4¼ oz/¾ cup) potato flour**

**175 g (6 oz/1 cup) rice flour**

**2 tsp gluten-free baking powder**

**85 g (3 oz) butter**

**3–4 tbsp milk**

**milk or water, for glazing**

**1 tbsp poppy seeds**

**Ricotta Filling**

**185 g (6½ oz/¾ cup) ricotta cheese**

**2 spring onions (scallions), finely
  chopped**

**Prep time** 20 minutes

**Cooking time** 15 minutes

**Serves** 4–6

**1**  Preheat the oven to 180°C (350°F/Gas 4). Lightly grease a 20 cm (8 in) sandwich tin.

**2**  Sift the dry ingredients into a bowl. Rub the butter in with your fingertips until the mixture resembles fine breadcrumbs. Make a well in the centre. Add enough milk to make a soft dough. Turn out onto a rice-floured board and knead lightly.

**3**  Roll the dough into a 5 mm (¼ in) thick rectangle between two sheets of baking paper. Turn and release the paper frequently to prevent the dough from sticking to the paper.

**4**  To make the ricotta filling, beat the ricotta cheese in a bowl until creamy. Add the spring onions and mix well. Spread the filling over the dough.

**5**  Use the baking paper to help you roll up the dough. Once you have a roll, cut it into 2 cm (¾ in) thick slices. Place the slices, cut side up, into the prepared tin. Glaze with milk or water and sprinkle the top with poppy seeds. Bake for 12–15 minutes. Serve hot or cold.

# Savoury flat bread

80 g (2¾ oz/½ cup) brown rice flour

55 g (2 oz/½ cup) arrowroot

¾ tsp bicarbonate of soda (baking soda)

1½ tsp cream of tartar

100 g (3½ oz/1 cup) rice bran

250 ml (9 fl oz/1 cup) chicken stock <sup>GF</sup> (Basics) or water

3 tbsp canola or olive oil

canola or olive oil, extra, for glazing

1 tbsp salt

1 tbsp poppy seeds

**1**  Preheat the oven to 190°C (375°F/Gas 5). Grease two
baking trays.

**2**  Sift the flour, arrowroot, bicarbonate of soda and cream
of tartar into a large bowl. Add the rice bran. Make a
well in the centre, then add the combined stock and oil.
Beat until smooth with a wooden spoon.

**3**  Spoon heaped tablespoons of the dough onto the
prepared trays.

**4**  Bake for 20 minutes. Remove from the oven, brush with
oil and sprinkle with salt and poppy seeds. Return to
the oven and bake for a further 15–20 minutes.

**Prep time** 20 minutes
**Cooking time** 40 minutes
**Makes** 6–8 rounds

nutrition per slice (10)   Energy **1495 kJ (357 Cal)** Fat **13.8 g** Saturated fat **2.6 g**
Protein **3.5 g** Carbohydrate **53.6 g** Fibre **1.2 g** Cholesterol **25 mg** Sodium **618 g**

# White bread

500 ml (17 fl oz/2 cups) milk

4 tsp dried yeast <sup>GF</sup>

1 tbsp sugar

550 g (1 lb 4 oz/3⅔ cups) gluten-free
plain (all-purpose) flour

2 tsp salt

4 tbsp canola or olive oil

1 egg

2 tbsp roasted buckwheat kernels
(groats) (optional)

2 tbsp canola or olive oil, extra,
for glazing

**Prep time** 40 minutes

**Cooking time** 55 minutes

**Serves** 8–10

**1**   Preheat the oven to 220°C (425°F/Gas 7). Lightly grease a 20 x 14 cm (8 x 5½ in) loaf tin.

**2**   Pour the milk into a saucepan over medium heat, bring almost to the boil, then remove from the heat and allow to cool until it is lukewarm.

**3**   Combine the yeast, sugar and the warm milk in a bowl, then stir to dissolve the yeast. Stand the bowl in a warm place for about 10 minutes, or until the mixture is frothy.

**4**   Sift the flour into a large bowl and add the salt. Make a well in the centre and add the yeast mixture, oil and egg. Beat well with a wooden spoon. Pour into the prepared tin and sprinkle with buckwheat, if using. Cover loosely and place in a warm place for about 20 minutes, or until the mixture comes to the top of the tin.

**5**   Bake for 20 minutes, then reduce the heat to 200°C (400°F/Gas 6) and bake for a further 30–35 minutes, or until cooked. Brush with the extra oil during cooking at least twice to help promote browning.

# Pikelets

**Prep time** 15 minutes
**Cooking time** 25 minutes
**Makes** about 24

115 g (4 oz/¾ cup) gluten-free plain (all-purpose) flour
½ tsp bicarbonate of soda (baking soda)
1 tsp cream of tartar
4 tbsp rice bran
2 eggs, separated
1 tbsp canola oil
strawberry jam <sup>GF</sup> (Basics), to serve

**1**  Sift the flour, bicarbonate of soda and cream of tartar
into a bowl. Mix in the rice bran. Make a well in the
centre. In a separate bowl, combine the egg yolks, oil
and 250 ml (9 fl oz/1 cup) water. Add to the well in the
dry ingredients. Beat well until smooth.

**2**  Beat the egg whites in the small bowl of an electric
mixer until stiff peaks form, then fold into the batter
using a large spoon.

**3**  Spray a non-stick frying pan lightly with canola or olive
oil and place over medium heat. Place tablespoonfuls of
the mixture in the pan, allowing room for spreading.
When the mixture starts to set and bubbles burst, turn
over and brown the other side. Place on a wire rack to
cool. Repeat with the remaining mixture. Serve the
warm pikelets topped with strawberry jam.

# Rhubarb muffins

**300 g (10½ oz/2 cups) gluten-free self-raising flour**

**2 tsp gluten-free baking powder**

**140 g (5 oz/¾ cup) soft brown sugar**

**185 ml (6 fl oz/¾ cup) milk**

**4 tbsp canola oil**

**2 eggs, lightly beaten**

**200 g (7 oz/½ bunch) trimmed rhubarb, washed and cut into 2 cm (3/4 in) pieces**

**Prep time** 15 minutes
**Cooking time** 20 minutes
**Makes** 12

**1** Preheat the oven to 180°C (350°F/Gas 4). Lightly grease 12 holes of a regular muffin tray.

**2** Sift the flour and baking powder into a large bowl. Stir in the sugar and make a well in the centre. In a separate bowl, combine the milk, oil and eggs. Pour into the well in the dry ingredients along with the rhubarb. Use a large metal spoon to mix until just combined. Divide the batter evenly among the prepared muffin holes.

**3** Bake for 18–20 minutes, or until a skewer inserted in the centre comes out clean. Leave to cool in the tin for 5 minutes before turning out onto a wire rack to cool completely.

## nutrition per muffin
Energy **948 kJ (226 Cal)** Fat **10 g** Saturated fat **1.5 g**
Protein **3.9 g** Carbohydrate **29.4 g** Fibre **3.8 g** Cholesterol **41 mg** Sodium **508 g**

# Savoury corn and chive muffins

300 g (10½ oz/2 cups) gluten-free
    self-raising flour

2 tsp gluten-free baking powder

2 tbsp soft brown sugar

100 g (3½ oz/½ cup) drained, tinned
    corn kernels

2 tbsp finely chopped fresh chives

250 ml (9 fl oz/1 cup) milk

4 tbsp canola or olive oil

2 eggs, lightly beaten

**Prep time** 15 minutes
**Cooking time** 20 minutes
**Makes** 10

1 Preheat the oven to 180°C (350°F/Gas 4). Lightly grease 10 holes of a regular muffin tin.

2 Sift the flour and baking powder into a large bowl. Stir in the sugar, corn and chives, then make a well in the centre. In a separate bowl, combine the milk, oil and eggs. Pour into the well in the dry ingredients. Use a large metal spoon to mix until just combined. Divide the batter evenly among the prepared muffin holes.

3 Bake for 18–20 minutes, or until a skewer inserted in the centre comes out clean. Leave in the tray for 5 minutes before turning out onto a wire rack to cool.

## nutrition per serve  Energy **475 kJ (113 Cal)**  Fat **3.6 g**  Saturated fat **0.4 g**
Protein **1.6 g**  Carbohydrate **18.3 g**  Fibre **0.9 g**  Cholesterol **19 mg**  Sodium **181 g**

# Apple slice

**220 g (7¾ oz/1½ cups) gluten-free self-raising flour**

**½ tsp gluten-free baking powder**

**175 g (6 oz/¾ cup) caster (superfine) sugar**

**2 eggs, lightly beaten**

**3 tbsp apple juice**

**3 tbsp canola oil**

**335 g (11¾ oz/1½ cups) unsweetened stewed apples**

**pure icing (confectioners') sugar GF, to serve**

**Prep time** 15 minutes
**Cooking time** 35 minutes
**Makes** about 20 pieces

**1**  Preheat the oven to 190°C (375°F/Gas 5). Lightly grease a 28 x 18 cm (11¼ x 7 in) baking tin and cover the base and two long sides with baking paper.

**2**  Sift the flour and baking powder into a bowl and add the sugar. Make a well in the centre. Combine the eggs, juice, oil and 125 ml (4 fl oz/½ cup) cold water in a separate bowl, then add to the dry ingredients. Mix until thoroughly combined.

**3**  Spread half the batter into the prepared tin. Spread the stewed apple carefully over the top, then spoon the remaining batter gently over the apple so that it is completely covered.

**4**  Bake for 30–35 minutes, or until golden. Cool slightly in the tin, then place on a wire rack to cool completely. Dust with icing sugar and cut into 20 pieces before serving.

# Patty cakes

125 g (4½ oz) butter

115 g (4 oz/½ cup) caster (superfine) sugar

2 eggs, or equivalent egg replacer

150 g (5½ oz/1 cup) gluten-free self-raising flour

90 g (3¼ oz/½ cup) rice flour

3 tsp gluten-free baking powder

125 ml (4 fl oz/½ cup) milk

pure icing (confectioners') sugar GF, for dusting

**1**  Preheat oven to 180°C (350°F/Gas 4). Line 12 holes of two regular muffin trays or patty pans with paper cases.

**2**  In the small bowl of an electric mixer, beat the butter and sugar together until light and fluffy. Add the eggs, one at a time, beating well after each addition.

**3**  Sift the dry ingredients into a large bowl. Fold the dry ingredients into the butter mixture alternately with the milk.

**4**  Spoon the mixture evenly into the muffin holes and bake for about 15–20 minutes, or until just cooked. Cool on a wire rack. Dust the patty cakes with pure icing sugar before serving.

**Prep time** 15 minutes
**Cooking time** 20 minutes
**Makes** 24

nutrition per serve (8)   Energy **1477 kJ (353 Cal)**  Fat **18.9 g**  Saturated fat **11.5 g**
Protein **4.3 g**  Carbohydrate **42.7 g**  Fibre **0.6 g**  Cholesterol **123 mg**  Sodium **334g**

# Sponge cake

**4 eggs**

**165 g (5¾ oz/¾ cup) sugar**

**150 g (5½ oz/1 cup) soy-free, gluten-free plain (all-purpose) flour, sifted**

**100 g (3½ oz/⅓ cup) strawberry jam ᴳᶠ (Basics)**

**pure icing (confectioners') sugar ᴳᶠ, to serve**

**300 ml (10½ fl oz) pouring (whipping) cream**

**Prep time** 20 minutes
**Cooking time** 30 minutes
**Serves** 6–8

**1**  Preheat the oven to 180°C (350°F/Gas 4). Lightly grease and flour two 20 cm (8 in) round cake tins, then line the base with baking paper.

**2**  Beat the eggs and sugar in the small bowl of an electric mixer for about 6–7 minutes, or until light and fluffy. Very gently fold the sifted flour into the egg mixture alternately with 4 tablespoons hot water. Gently spread the mixture into the prepared pans.

**3**  Bake for about 25–30 minutes, or until lightly browned and the cakes have slightly left the side of the tins. Turn onto a wire rack to cool.

**4**  Whip the cream into stiff peaks.

**5**  Spread the jam over the top of one sponge, and top with the cream. Place the other sponge on top and dust with icing sugar.

# Bread rolls

4 tsp dried yeast <sup>GF</sup>

1 tbsp soft brown sugar

2 tsp guar gum or xanthan gum

300 g (10½ oz/2 cups) gluten-free plain (all-purpose) flour

135 g (4¾ oz/¾ cup) rice flour

2 tsp salt

40 g (1½ oz/½ cup) rice bran

60 g (2¼ oz) butter, melted, cooled

2 tbsp poppy seeds or sesame seeds (optional)

canola or olive oil, for brushing

## nutrition per roll
Energy **1300 kJ (311 Cal)** Fat **10.4 g** Saturated fat **4.6 g**
Protein **3.1 g** Carbohydrate **48.8 g** Fibre **3.3 g** Cholesterol **19 mg** Sodium **1334 g**

**Prep time** 40 minutes +
rising time
**Cooking time** 35 minutes
**Makes** 8

**1** Preheat the oven to 200°C (400°F/Gas 6). Lightly grease eight 10 x 5.5 cm (4 x 2¼ in) individual loaf tins.

**2** Combine the yeast, sugar and 500 ml (17 fl oz/2 cups) warm water in a bowl, then stir to dissolve the yeast. Stand the bowl in a warm place for about 10 minutes, or until the mixture is frothy.

**3** Sift the gum and flours into a large bowl. Add the salt and rice bran. Make a well in the centre and add the yeast mixture and cooled butter. Mix well to form a soft dough. Divide into eight equal portions, then gently shape with gluten-free floured hands into an oval shape. Place in the prepared tins. Sprinkle with poppy seeds or sesame seeds, if using.

**4** Cover tins loosely and leave in a warm place for 45–60 minutes, or until mixture comes to top of tins.

**5** Bake for 25–30 minutes, or until cooked through. Brush with oil during cooking at least twice to help promote browning. Remove from the tins and leave to cool on a wire rack.

# Flourless chocolate walnut cake

**125 g (4½ oz/1¼ cups) walnuts**

**250 g (9 oz) dark chocolate** <sup>GF</sup>**,
   chopped**

**2 tbsp pouring (whipping) cream**

**1 tsp natural vanilla extract**

**115 g (4 oz/½ cup) caster (superfine)
   sugar**

**6 eggs, separated**

**fresh raspberries, to serve**

**whipped cream, to serve**

**Prep time** 20 minutes
**Cooking time** 40 minutes
**Serves** 8

**1**  Preheat oven to 180°C (350°F/Gas 4). Grease and line the base of a 20 cm (8 in) spring-form cake tin with baking paper.

**2**  Process walnuts in a food processor until finely ground.

**3**  Put the chocolate, cream and vanilla extract in a heatproof bowl. Sit over a saucepan half filled with simmering water. Turn off the heat and stir the chocolate until just melted. Allow the mixture to cool a little.

**4**  Add the sugar, egg yolks and ground walnuts to the chocolate mixture and mix to combine. Using electric beaters, beat the egg whites until firm peaks form. Stir a large spoonful of the egg white into the chocolate to soften the mixture, then fold through the remaining egg white. Pour into the prepared tin. Bake for 40 minutes or until firm to touch. Leave to cool for 5 minutes, then turn out onto a wire rack to cool completely. Serve with fresh raspberries and whipped cream.

# Banana loaf

300 g (10½ oz/2 cups) gluten-free
  self-raising flour

2 tsp gluten-free baking powder

125 g (4½ oz/⅔ cup) soft brown sugar

¼ tsp ground cinnamon

125 g (4½ oz) butter, melted, cooled slightly

125 ml (4 fl oz/½ cup) milk

2 eggs

3 large (700 g/1 lb 9 oz) ripe bananas, mashed

butter, to serve

maple syrup, to serve

**1**  Preheat the oven to 170°C (325°F/Gas 3). Grease a
  21 x 11 cm (8¼ x 4¼ in) loaf tin. Line the base of the
  tin with baking paper.

**2**  Sift the flour, baking powder, sugar and cinnamon into
  a large bowl. In a separate bowl, whisk the butter, milk
  and egg together. Add the milk mixture to the dry
  ingredients with the mashed bananas. Use a wooden
  spoon to mix until well combined.

**3**  Pour the mixture into the prepared tin and smooth the
  surface with a spoon. Bake for 40 minutes, or until a
  skewer inserted into the centre comes out clean. Set
  aside in the tin for 5 minutes before turning out onto a
  wire rack to cool. Serve warm or at room temperature.
  Cut into slices, spread with butter and drizzle with a
  little maple syrup.

**Prep time** 20 minutes
**Cooking time** 50 minutes
**Serves** 8

**nutrition per scone**  Energy **999 kJ (239 Cal)**  Fat **6.8 g**  Saturated fat **4.3 g**
Protein **1.6 g**  Carbohydrate **42.7 g**  Fibre **4.8 g**  Cholesterol **20 mg**  Sodium **23 g**

# Scones

550 g (1 lb 4 oz/3⅔ cups) gluten-free
  self-raising flour

3 tsp gluten-free baking powder

80 g (2¾ oz) butter, softened

1 tbsp caster (superfine) sugar

310 ml (10¾ fl oz/1¼ cups) milk

whipped cream, to serve

strawberry jam ᴳᶠ (Basics), to serve


**Prep time** 10 minutes
**Cooking time** 15 minutes
**Makes** 12

**1** Preheat the oven to 220°C (425°F/Gas 7). Line a baking tray with a sheet of baking paper.

**2** Sift the flour, baking powder and a pinch of salt into a large bowl. Use your fingertips to rub the butter into the flour until it resembles fine breadcrumbs. Stir in the sugar. Add the milk and use a round-bladed knife to mix until the dough just comes together.

**3** Turn out onto a surface lightly dusted with gluten-free flour and knead until combined. Press or roll out until the dough is about 2 cm (¾ in) thick. Use a 5.5 cm (2¼ in) round cutter to cut out the dough. Place on the lined tray about 1 cm (½ in) apart. Re-roll and cut any remaining dough.

**4** Bake for 12–15 minutes, or until cooked. Serve warm with lashings of whipped cream and strawberry jam.

**nutrition per cookie**  Energy **311 kJ (74 Cal)** Fat **3.2 g** Saturated fat **2 g**
Protein **0.4 g** Carbohydrate **11.2 g** Fibre **0.2 g** Cholesterol **10 mg** Sodium **2 g**

# Jam cookies

90 g (3¼ oz) unsalted butter

110 g (3¾ oz/½ cup) sugar

125 g (4½ oz/¾ cup) rice flour

¼ tsp gluten-free baking powder

165 g (53/4 oz/½ cup) strawberry jam <sup>GF</sup> (Basics)

**Prep time** 20 minutes
**Cooking time** 15 minutes
**Makes** about 24

**1**  Preheat the oven to 190°C (375°F/Gas 5). Lightly grease two baking trays.

**2**  Use electric beaters to beat the butter and sugar until light and fluffy. Sift in the flour and baking powder, then stir together. Add 1 tablespoon water and stir until well blended and a dough forms.

**3**  Shape the dough into walnut-sized balls, then space them out on the prepared baking trays—you should have about 24 balls.

**4**  Make an indentation in each cookie using the handle of a wooden spoon. Put ¼ teaspoon jam in each biscuit. Bake for 10–15 minutes, or until light golden. Cool on wire racks.

## nutrition per serve (10)   Energy **1348 kJ (322 Cal)** Fat **14.7 g** Saturated fat **9.1 g**
Protein **4.1 g** Carbohydrate **44.1 g** Fibre **1 g** Cholesterol **112 mg** Sodium **330 g**

# Pumpkin and coconut tart

1 quantity gluten-free sweet
   shortcrust pastry (Basics)

375 g (13 oz/1½ cups) cooked
   mashed butternut pumpkin
   (squash)

3 eggs, lightly beaten

165 g (5¾ oz/¾ cup firmly packed)
   soft brown sugar

125 g (4½ oz/½ cup) sour cream

30 g (1 oz/½ cup) flaked coconut

3 tbsp golden syrup or pure maple
   syrup

pure icing (confectioners') sugar GF,
   to dust

**Prep time** 25 minutes
**Cooking time** 1¼ hours
**Serves** 8–10

**1** Preheat the oven to 200°C (400°F/Gas 6). Lightly grease a 23 cm (9 in) loose-based flan tin.

**2** Roll out the pastry between two sheets of baking paper until large enough to line the prepared tin. Reserve any leftover dough.

**3** Place the tin on a baking tray. Cover the pastry with a sheet of crumpled baking paper and fill with baking beads or rice. Bake for 10 minutes. Remove the beads and paper and bake for a further 10–15 minutes, or until lightly browned. Fill any cracks with small amounts of reserved pastry. Bake for a further 2 minutes to set. Remove from the oven and cool completely. Reduce the oven temperature to 180°C (350°F/Gas 4).

**4** To make the filling, combine all the ingredients (except the icing sugar) in a large bowl and mix together well. Place the cooled pastry case on a baking tray and pour in the filling.

**5** Bake for 45 minutes; or until the filling is just set. Cool completely before serving. Dust the edges lightly with icing sugar.

# Mixed berry muffins

300 g (10½ oz/2 cups) gluten-free
plain (all-purpose) flour

1 tbsp gluten-free baking powder

25 g (1 oz/½ cup) baby rice cereal
or rice porridge

150 g (5½ oz/⅔ cup) caster
(superfine) sugar

2 eggs, lightly beaten

375 ml (13 fl oz/1½ cups) reduced-
fat milk

2 tbsp canola oil

250 g (9 oz/1⅔ cups) fresh or frozen
mixed berries

**1**  Preheat oven to 200°C (400°F/Gas 6). Lightly grease
12 holes of a regular muffin tray.

**2**  Sift the flour and baking powder into a large bowl. Stir
in the rice cereal and sugar and make a well in the
centre. In a separate bowl combine the beaten eggs,
milk and oil. Pour the mixture into the well in the dry
ingredients and stir briefly until the batter is just
incorporated. Quickly and lightly stir through the
berries. Do not over-mix. Divide the batter evenly
among the prepared muffin holes.

**3**  Bake for 20 minutes, or until golden brown and risen.
Leave in the tray for 5 minutes before turning out onto
a wire rack to cool completely.

**Prep time** 15 minutes
**Cooking time** 20 minutes
**Makes** 12

# Vanilla cookies

125 g (4½ oz) unsalted butter

4 tbsp caster (superfine) sugar

1 tsp natural vanilla extract

150 g (5½ oz/1 cup) gluten-free plain (all-purpose) flour

70 g (2½ oz/½ cup) gluten-free
   self-raising flour

**Prep time** 15 minutes
**Cooking time** 15 minutes
**Makes** about 18

1   Preheat the oven to 170°C (325°F/Gas 3). Line two baking trays with baking paper.

2   Beat the butter, sugar and vanilla extract in the small bowl of an electric mixer for 1–2 minutes, or until well combined. Sift the flours into the butter mixture. Use a wooden spoon to mix until well combined. Use your hands to shape the mixture into a soft dough.

3   Shape tablespoons of the mixture into balls and place on the prepared trays. Use a fork to flatten the balls until about 1 cm (⅜ in) thick. Bake for 12–15 minutes, swapping the trays around once, until light golden. Transfer the cookies to a wire rack to cool.

nutrition per serve   Energy **661 kJ (158 Cal)**  Fat **3.2 g**  Saturated fat **1 g**
Protein **4.1 g** Carbohydrate **29.3 g** Fibre **0.1 g** Cholesterol **119 mg** Sodium **45 g**

# Coffee mousse meringue roll

**Coffee Mousse**

**4 egg yolks**

**3 tbsp sugar**

**3 tsp pure maize cornflour (cornstarch)** GF

**1½ tsp instant coffee powder**

**pure maize cornflour (cornstarch)** GF, **for dusting**

**4 egg whites**

**110 g (3¾ oz/½ cup) sugar**

**2 tsp pure maize cornflour (cornstarch)** GF

**pure icing (confectioners') sugar** GF, **for dusting**

**Prep time** 35 minutes
**Cooking time** 15 minutes
**Serves** 4–6

**1**  To make the coffee mousse, beat the egg yolks and sugar in the small bowl of an electric mixer until thick and creamy. In a separate small bowl, blend the cornflour, coffee powder and 185 ml (6 fl oz/¾ cup) water. Add to the egg mixture. Transfer to a saucepan and stir over low heat until the mixture boils and thickens. Pour the mixture into a bowl. Cover with plastic wrap and chill well before using.

**2**  Preheat the oven to 200°C (400°F/Gas 6). Lightly grease a 25 x 30 cm (10 x 12 in) Swiss roll (jelly roll) tin, line with baking paper, grease again and dust with cornflour.

**3**  Beat the egg whites until light and fluffy. Gradually beat in the sugar and continue beating until the meringue is stiff and glossy. Gently fold in the cornflour. Spread the meringue mixture evenly into the prepared Swiss roll tin, using a spatula.

**4**  Bake for 12–15 minutes, or until the meringue has risen and is golden brown. Quickly turn out onto a sheet of baking paper that has been coated with sifted pure icing sugar. Allow to cool until lukewarm.

**5**  Spread the mousse over the meringue. Roll up from the short side using the baking paper as a guide. Place on a chilled platter. Refrigerate the roll until ready to serve, then slice.

## nutrition per meringue

Energy **128 kJ (31 Cal)** Fat **0 g** Saturated fat **0 g**
Protein **0.3 g** Carbohydrate **7.6 g** Fibre **0 g** Cholesterol **0 mg** Sodium **6 g**

# Meringue kisses

**pure maize cornflour (cornstarch)** GF, for dusting

**2 egg whites**

**150 g (5½ oz/⅔ cup) caster (superfine) sugar**

**1 tsp pure icing (confectioners') sugar** GF

**Prep time** 20 minutes
**Cooking time** 40 minutes
**Makes** about 20

**1**  Preheat the oven to 120°C (235°F/Gas ½). Lightly grease two baking trays, then dust them lightly with cornflour.

**2**  Combine the egg whites, caster sugar and a pinch of salt in the small bowl of an electric mixer. Beat on high speed for 10–12 minutes. Gently fold in the icing sugar.

**3**  Spoon the meringue into a piping bag fitted with a fluted tube. Pipe stars or rosettes onto the prepared trays. Bake for about 40 minutes, or until the meringues feel firm and dry. Leave to cool in the oven with the door ajar.

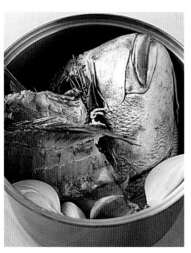

# Basics

# Beef stock

**2 kg (4 lb 8 oz) beef bones**

**2 unpeeled carrots, chopped**

**2 unpeeled onions, quartered**

**2 tbsp tomato paste (concentrated purée)** <sup>GF</sup>

**2 celery stalks, leaves included, chopped**

**1 bouquet garni**

**12 black peppercorns**

**1** Preheat the oven to 210°C (415°F/Gas 6–7). Put the bones in a baking tin and bake for 30 minutes, turning occasionally. Add the carrot and onion and cook for a further 20 minutes. Allow to cool.

**2** Put the bones, onion and carrot in a large, heavy-based saucepan. Drain the excess fat from baking tin and pour 250 ml (9 fl oz/ 1 cup) water into the tin. Stir to dissolve any pan juices, then add the liquid to the pan.

**3** Add the tomato paste, celery and 2.5 litres (87 fl oz/10 cups) water. Bring to the boil, skimming the surface as required, and then add the bouquet garni and peppercorns. Reduce the heat to low and simmer gently for 4 hours. Skim the froth from the surface regularly.

**4** Strain through a colander, then through a fine sieve. Remove any fat from the surface. Store in the refrigerator for up to 2 days or in the freezer for up to 6 months.

**Makes** about 1.75 litres (61 fl oz/7 cups)

# Chicken stock

**2 kg (4 lb 8 oz) chicken bones**

**2 unpeeled onions, quartered**

**2 unpeeled carrots, chopped**

**2 celery stalks, leaves included, chopped**

**1 bouquet garni**

**12 black peppercorns**

**1** Put the chicken bones, onion, carrot, celery and 3.5 litres (122 fl oz/14 cups) water in a large, heavy-based saucepan. Bring slowly to the boil. Skim the surface as required and add the bouquet garni and peppercorns. Reduce the heat to low and simmer gently for 3 hours. Skim the froth from the surface regularly.

**2** Strain the stock. Set aside to cool, then refrigerate until cold. Spoon off any fat that has set on the surface. Transfer to an airtight container. Store in the refrigerator for up to 2 days or in the freezer for up to 6 months.

**Makes** about 2.5 litres (87 fl oz/10 cups)

# Vegetable stock

1 tbsp oil

1 onion, chopped

2 leeks, thickly sliced

4 carrots, chopped

2 parsnips, chopped

4 celery stalks, leaves included, chopped

2 bay leaves

1 bouquet garni

4 unpeeled garlic cloves

8 black peppercorns

**1** Heat the oil in a large, heavy-based saucepan and add the onion, leek, carrot, parsnip and celery. Cover and cook for 5 minutes without colouring. Add 3 litres (105 fl oz/12 cups) water. Bring to the boil. Add the bay leaves, bouquet garni, garlic and peppercorns. Reduce the heat to low and simmer for 1 hour. Skim the froth from the surface of the stock regularly.

**2** Strain the stock. Set aside to cool, then transfer to an airtight container. Store in the refrigerator for up to 2 days or in the freezer for up to 6 months.

**Makes** about 2.5 litres (87 fl oz/10 cups)

# Fish stock

2 kg (4 lb 8 oz) chopped fish bones, heads and tails

1 celery stalk, leaves included, roughly chopped

1 onion, chopped

1 unpeeled carrot, chopped

1 leek, sliced

1 bouquet garni

12 black peppercorns

**1** Place the fish bones, celery, onion, carrot, leek and 2 litres (70 fl oz/8 cups) of water in a large, heavy-based saucepan. Bring slowly to the boil. Skim the surface as required and add the bouquet garni and peppercorns. Reduce the heat to low and simmer very gently for 20 minutes. Skim off any froth regularly.

**2** Ladle the stock in batches into a sieve lined with damp muslin sitting over a bowl. To keep a clear fish stock, do not press the solids, but simply allow the stock to strain undisturbed. Allow to cool, then store in the refrigerator for up to 2 days, or in the freezer for up to 6 months.

**Makes** about 1.75 litres (61 fl oz/7 cups)

# French dressing (vinaigrette)

**3 tbsp olive oil**
**2 tbsp white wine vinegar**
**1 tsp wholegrain mustard**
**freshly ground pepper, to taste**

**1**  Place all the ingredients in a small screw-top jar and shake well. Use immediately.

**Makes** about 125 ml (4 fl oz/½ cup)

# Italian dressing

**3 tbsp white wine vinegar**
**3 tbsp olive oil**
**½ tsp sugar**
**1 tbsp chopped fresh basil**

**1**  Put the vinegar, olive oil and sugar in a bowl and whisk to combine. Stir in the basil and leave to stand for 15 minutes before serving.

**Makes** about 125 ml (4 fl oz/½ cup)

# Mayonnaise

2 egg yolks

¼ tsp salt

250 ml (9 fl oz/1 cup) canola oil

½ tsp lemon juice

**1** Put the egg yolks and salt in a bowl and whisk together until well combined and thick.

**2** Gradually whisk in the oil, drop by drop, from a teaspoon until a quarter of the oil has been added. The mixture should be thick at this stage. Very slowly pour in the remaining oil in a thick steady stream, while continuing to beat steadily. Beat in the lemon juice. Store in a glass jar in the refrigerator for up to 3 days.

**Makes** about 250 ml (9 fl oz/1 cup)

# Mango chutney

1 tbsp oil

2 garlic cloves, crushed

1 tsp grated ginger

2 cinnamon sticks

4 cloves

½ tsp chilli powder

1 kg (2 lb 4 oz) fresh or frozen ripe mango flesh, roughly chopped

375 ml (13 fl oz/1½ cups) white vinegar

250 g (9 oz/heaped 1 cup) caster (superfine) sugar

**1** Heat the oil in a heavy-based saucepan over medium heat, add the garlic and ginger and fry for 1 minute. Add the remaining ingredients and bring to the boil.

**2** Reduce the heat to low and cook for 1 hour, or until the mango is thick and pulpy, like jam. It should fall in sheets off the spoon when it is ready. Add salt, to taste, and more chilli if you wish. Remove the whole spices.

**3** Pour the chutney into hot sterilized jars (wash the jars in boiling water and dry them thoroughly in a warm oven). Seal the jars and allow to cool completely. Store in a cool place or in the refrigerator after opening.

**Makes** about 500 ml (17 fl oz/2 cups)

# Basic tomato sauce

1.5 kg (3 lb 5 oz) tomatoes

1 tbsp olive oil

1 onion, finely chopped

2 garlic cloves, crushed

2 tbsp tomato paste (concentrated purée) GF

1 tsp dried oregano

1 tsp dried basil

1 tsp sugar

**1** Score a cross on the base of each tomato, place in a bowl of boiling water for 10 seconds, then plunge into cold water and peel away the skin from the cross. Finely chop the flesh.

**2** Heat the oil in a saucepan. Add the onion and cook, stirring, over medium heat for 3 minutes, or until soft. Add the garlic and cook for 1 minute. Add the tomato, tomato paste, oregano, basil and sugar. Bring to the boil, then reduce the heat and simmer for 20 minutes, or until the sauce has thickened slightly. Store in an airtight container in the refrigerator for up to 2 days or in the freezer for up to 6 months.

**Makes** about 1.5 litres (52 fl oz/6 cups)

# Strawberry jam

1.25 kg (2 lb 12 oz/5⅔ cups) sugar

1.5 kg (3 lb 5 oz) strawberries

125 ml (4 fl oz/½ cup) lemon juice

**1** Warm the sugar by spreading in a large baking dish and heating in an oven preheated to 120°C (235°F/Gas ½) for 10 minutes, stirring occasionally. Put two plates in the freezer. Hull the strawberries and put in a large pan with the lemon juice, sugar and 125 ml (4 fl oz/½ cup) water. Warm gently, without boiling, stirring carefully with a wooden spoon. Try not to break up the fruit too much.

**2** Increase the heat and, without boiling, continue stirring for 10 minutes, until sugar has thoroughly dissolved. Increase heat and boil, without stirring, for 20 minutes. Start testing for the setting point: place a little jam on one of the cold plates, a skin will form on the surface and the jam will wrinkle when pushed with a finger. It could take up to 40 minutes to reach setting point. Remove from the heat and leave for 5 minutes before removing any scum that forms on the surface. Pour into hot sterilized jars, seal and label.

**Makes** about 1 litre (35 fl oz/4 cups)

# Shortcrust pastry

**190 g (6¾ oz/1¼ cups) gluten-free plain (all-purpose) flour**
**90 g (3¼ oz) cold butter, chopped**
**1 egg, lightly beaten**

## Food Processor Method

Put the flour and butter in a food processor and pulse until crumb-like. Add the egg and 1–2 teaspoons water until the dough is starting to come together. Don't add any more water than necessary. Turn out onto a surface lightly dusted with gluten-free flour and knead briefly to bring together the dough into a smooth ball. Wrap in plastic wrap and refrigerate to firm. Knead the dough well to help the dough hold together. Roll out between two sheets of baking paper that have been lightly dusted with gluten-free flour until large enough to line the prepared tin or dish. Refrigerate the lined dish for 30 minutes to prevent shrinkage and cracking.

## Bowl method

Sift the flour into a large bowl. Rub the butter into the flour with your fingertips until the mixture resembles dry breadcrumbs. Make a well in the centre and add the egg and 1–2 teaspoons water until the dough is starting to come together. Don't add any more water than necessary. Turn out onto a surface lightly dusted with gluten-free flour and knead briefly to bring together the dough into a smooth ball. Wrap in plastic wrap and refrigerate to firm. Roll out between two sheets of baking paper that have been lightly dusted with gluten-free flour until large enough to line the prepared tin or dish. Refrigerate the lined dish for 30 minutes to prevent shrinkage and cracking.

# Sweet shortcrust pastry

**190 g (6¾ oz/1¼ cups) gluten-free plain (all-purpose) flour**

**3 tbsp pure icing confectioners' sugar** GF

**90 g (3¼ oz) cold butter, chopped**

**1 egg, lightly beaten**

## Food Processor method

Put the flour and icing sugar in a food processor and briefly pulse to combine. Add the butter and pulse until crumb-like. Add the egg and 1–2 teaspoons water until the dough is starting to come together. Don't add any more water than necessary. Turn out onto a surface lightly dusted with gluten-free flour and knead briefly to bring together the dough into a smooth ball. Wrap in plastic wrap and refrigerate to firm. Knead the dough well to help the dough hold together. Roll out between two sheets of baking paper that have been lightly dusted with gluten-free flour until large enough to line the prepared tin or dish. Refrigerate lined dish for 30 minutes to prevent shrinkage and cracking.

## Bowl method

Sift the flour and icing (confectioners') sugar into a large bowl. Rub the butter into the flour with your fingertips until the mixture resembles dry breadcrumbs. Make a well in the centre and add egg and 1–2 teaspoons water until the dough is starting to come together. Don't add any more water than necessary. Turn out onto a surface lightly dusted with gluten-free flour and knead briefly to bring together the dough into a smooth ball. Wrap in plastic wrap and refrigerate to firm. Roll out between two sheets of baking paper that have been lightly dusted with gluten-free flour until large enough to line the prepared tin or dish. Refrigerate the lined dish for 30 minutes to prevent shrinkage and cracking.

Contact information for coeliac/dermatitis herpetiformis support groups

## AUSTRALIA

The Coeliac Society of Australia Inc
PO Box 271
Wahroonga, NSW, 2076
Phone: 02 9487 5088
Email: info@coeliacsociety.com.au
Internet: www.coeliacsociety.com.au

## CANADA

Canadian Celiac Association
5025 Orbitor Drive, Building 1, Ste 400
Mississauga, ON L4W 4Y5
Phone: 905 507 6208
Email: info@celiac.ca
Internet: www.celiac.ca

## GREAT BRITAIN

3rd Floor, Apollo Centre
Desborough Road
High Wycombe, Bucks HP11 2QW
Phone: 0845 305 2060
Internet: www.coeliac.org.uk

## NEW ZEALAND

Coeliac New Zealand (Inc)
P O Box 35724
Browns Bay
North Shore City 0753
Auckland
Phone: 09 820 5157
Email: admin@coeliac.co.nz
Internet: www.coeliac.co.nz

## USA

Celiac Disease Foundation
13251 Ventura Blvd, Ste 1
Studio City, CA 91604
Phone: 818 990 2354
Internet: www.celiac.org

# Index